Teach a Student to Spell: Level 1

Teach a Student to Spell: Level 1

By

Heather Marie Kosur

Rock Pickle Publishing

About the Workbook

The primary function of English spelling is to represent meaning. Spelling is not just sounds written down. The spelling of a word reflects its meaning, parts, history, relatives, and finally sounds.

Teach a Student to Spell: Level 1 is the follow-up workbook to the Teach a Student to Read reading program, which strives to teach students accurate and complete information about the English spelling system.

Instead of only learning spelling through rote memorization, students will learn the reasons for the spellings of words. Teach a Student to Spell teaches that sometimes every letter in a word spells a sound but that some letters do not spell sounds. Units of one, two, or three letters called graphemes (digraphs, trigraphs) spell sounds. Letters can be zeroed. Letters can be phonological, etymological, and/or lexical markers.

Level 1 consists of 36 spelling lists of 8 to 10 words each. The spelling lists are based on the most common words in English and various sight word lists. The goal of Level 1 is to teach the spellings of the most common English words and common English bases. Each list reinforces the graphemes taught in Teach a Student to Read. Some complex words are also introduced. Related words are noted.

Students must be early readers. Some knowledge of the English writing system such as the letters of the alphabet is required. Level 1 is recommended for ages 5 to 7 in kindergarten through first grade.

Acknowledgments

I could never express my full gratitude to Gina Cooke of Linguist-Educator Exchange (LEX) and Shameless Spelling. Without her materials and classes, I could not have gained a more accurate and complete understanding of the English spelling system for myself nor could I have facilitated my second-born in gaining the same knowledge. I owe her LEX Grapheme Deck and LEX InSight Word Decks endless thanks.

I highly recommend using the LEX Grapheme Deck and LEX InSight Word Decks as additional materials along with this reading program. I used both extensively while teaching my children to read and spell. The LEX Grapheme Deck contains even more information about English graphemes. I keep mine next to my workspace at all times for quick and easy reference. LEX InSight Word Decks provide detailed information about many common English words.

The LEX Grapheme Deck is available online: https://linguisteducatorexchange.com/lex-store/lex-grapheme-deck/

The LEX InSight Decks are available online: https://linguisteducatorexchange.com/lex-store/lex-insight-words/

Before You Begin

What is a letter? A letter is a character or symbol in an alphabet. When you learned your ABCs, you learned the letters of the alphabet. Letters are the raw materials for making graphemes and markers.

What is a grapheme? A grapheme is the "smallest meaningful contrastive unit in a writing system." The base <graph> denotes "write" An autograph is written in your own hand. A photograph is a picture written down. Graphemes are written. Graphemes are made of letters.

<h>, <sh>, and <ugh> are examples of graphemes. Single letters can be graphemes. Graphemes can be made of two letters. A two-letter grapheme is called a digraph. The morpheme <di> can denote "two" like in carbon dioxide. Graphemes can be made of three letters. A three-letter grapheme is called a trigraph. The morpheme <tri> can denote "three" like in tricycle or triceratops. In other words, a grapheme is one, two, or three letters that spell a phone.

A consonant cluster is a group of consonants without an intervening vowel.

Graphemes cannot cross morphemic boundaries. A morpheme is the smallest meaningful linguistic unit of a language. You can think of a morpheme as a word part that consists of one or more graphemes. A morpheme is a word part. Morphemes are made of graphemes. Bases, prefixes, suffixes, and connecting vowels are morphemes. A morphemic boundary is where two morphemes meet, like a window is the boundary between inside and outside. In other words, morphemes are building blocks of words.

In English, bases, prefixes, suffixes, and connecting vowels are types of morphemes. A base is a morpheme that forms the foundation of a word. A base holds the key to the meaning of the word that contains the base. A free base is a morpheme that can stand on its own as a word. The word <cat> is a free base. <cat> is a word on its own. <cat> is also the base of words like <cats> and <catty>. A bound base must attach to another morpheme to create a word. The <mit> in words like <emit>, <permit>, and <transmit> is a bound base. <mit> is a base that cannot be a word on its own. Every word has a base or is a base.

Other bound morphemes are prefixes and suffixes. Prefixes and suffixes are types of affixes. Affixes are bound morphemes by definition. A prefix is a bound morpheme that goes at the beginning of another morpheme. The <e> of <emit> is a prefix. A suffix is a bound morpheme that goes on the end of another morpheme. The <s> of <cats> is a suffix. The word <action> consists of two morphemes. <act> is a free base (free morpheme). <ion> is a suffix (bound morpheme). -*tion is not a suffix. <*ti> is not a morpheme. The <t> goes with <act>, and the <i> goes with <ion>. Graphemes cannot cross the boundaries of morphemes.

A connecting vowel is a <e>, <i>, <o>, or <u> that joins together two morphemes. The <o> in <geosphere> is a connecting vowel that links the base <ge> to the base <sphere>. We know that the <o> is a connecting vowel and that <ge> is a base because of the related word <geode>. <geode> is made of the base <ge> and the suffix <ode>. Connecting vowels are also bound morphemes.

Words are made of morphemes. Morphemes are made of graphemes. Graphemes are made of letters.

IPA Notation

The International Phonetic Association developed the IPA as a standardized representation of the sounds of spoken language. The phones and phonemes in this grammar are written using the IPA.

	Consonants								
				Place					
	Manner	Voicing	Bilabial	Labiodental	Dental	Alveolar	Palatal	Velar	Glottal
Obstruents	Stop	Voiceless	p			t		k	ʔ
		Voiced	b			d		g	
	Flap	Voiced				ɾ			
	Fricative	Voiceless		f	θ	s	ʃ	x	h
		Voiced		v	ð	z	ʒ		
	Affricate	Voiceless					t͡ʃ		
		Voiced					d͡ʒ		
Sonorants	Nasal	Voiced	m			n		ŋ	
	Liquid — Lateral	Voiced				l			
	Liquid — Rhotic	Voiced					ɹ		
	Glide	Voiced	w				j		

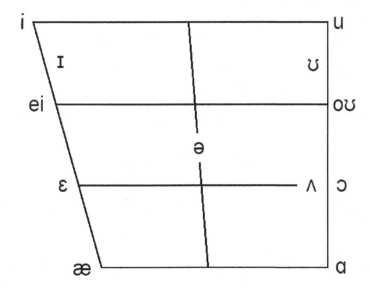

Phones

A phone is a distinct speech sound. Phones come out of your mouth. Phones are enclosed in square brackets. If you are unfamiliar with IPA, the words after each phone illustrate the sound each symbol represents.

[Ø]	no sound (zero phone)
[æ]	vowel in CAT, HAM, SAD <a>
[eɪ]	vowel in ATE, MAY, HEY, WEIGH, GREAT <ea>, <a>, <ay>, <ey>, <ai>, <e>, <ei>, <ee>
[ɑ]	vowel in HOT, SOCK <o>, BALL, FATHER, CAUGHT <a>, <oa>, <au>, <aw>, <eau>
[ɔ]	vowel in BALL, CAUGHT in Englishes without the cot-caught merger <o>, <a>, <oa>, <au>, <aw> (In Englishes with the cot-caught merger, see [ɑ].)
[b]	first sound in BIG, BALL <b>
[tʃ]	first sound in CHAIR, last sound in CATCH <ch>, <tch>, <t>, <c>
[d]	first sound in DAD, DO, DUCK <d>, <dh>
[ɛ]	vowel in JET, WET, LEG <e>, <ea>, <ei>, <ae>, <ai>, <ay>
[i]	vowel in ME, SEE, SEA, final vowel in FUNNY, WINDY <e>, <ee>, <ea>, <ey>, <ie>, <y>, <i>, <ei>, <ae>, <oe>
[f]	first sound in FISH, FAST <f>, <v>, <ugh>, <ph> <p> <pf>
[g]	first sound in GET, GOAT, GONE <g>, <gu>, <gh>
[gz]	<x> in EXACTLY <x>
[gʒ]	<x> in LUXURY <x>
[h]	first sound in HAS, HAT <h>, <wh>, <ch>, <j>, <x>
[ç]	first sound in HEAT, HUMID <h>
[x]	first sound in HANUKKAH, CHANUKAH, KHAT, last sound in LOCH <h>, <ch>, <kh>, <q>, <j>, <x>
[ɪ]	vowel in IN, DID, WITH <i>, <y>
[ɑɪ]	vowel sound in I, MINE, MY EYE <i>, <y>, <igh>, <ey>, <ai>, <ei>, <ae>, <ay>
[dʒ]	first sound in JET, JOKE, last sound in FUDGE <j>, <g>, <dg>, <d>
[ʒ]	first sound in GENRE, middle sound in CLOSURE, AZURE, last sound in BEIGE <s>, <g>, <z>, <j>
[k]	first and last sound in KICK, first sound in CAT, last sound in BISQUE, ZUCCHINI <c>, <k>, <ck>, <qu>, <cch>, <ch>, <kh>, <q>
[kw]	initial sound in QUIT, QUIET <qu>
[ks]	last sound in AX, OX <x>
[kʃ]	<x> in ANXIOUS <x>
[l]	first sound in LAD, the last sound in CALL <l>
[lj]	<gl> in IMBROGLIO, INTAGLIO
[m]	first sound in ME, MAT <m>, last sound in TOMB <mb>
[m̩]	last sound in RHYTHM <m>
[n]	first sound in NOT, NO, KNIT, GNAW <n>, <kn>, <gn>
[nj]	first sound in GNOCCHI, last consonant in LASAGNA <gn>
[ŋ]	last sound in RING, RANG <n>
[oʊ]	vowel diphthong in NO, GOAT, RODE, BUREAU <o>, <oa>, <ow>, <oe>, <eau>, <au>
[ʊ]	vowel in GOOD, BOOK, PUT <oo>, <ou>, <u>, <o>
[ɔɪ]	vowel in TOY, OIL <oy>, <oi>, <eu>
[aʊ]	vowel diphthong in COW, ABOUT <ow>, <ou>, <au>, <ao>
[p]	first sound in PIG, PICKLE, PLUMP <p>
[ɹ]	first sound in RAT, READ, WRITE <r>, <wr>, <rh>, <rrh>
[s]	first sound in SIT, SEE, CITY <s>, <c>, <z>, <sc>, <ps>, <ts>
[ʃ]	first sound in SHE, SHELL <sh>, <s>, <ch>, <t>, <c>, <sc>, <sch>
[t]	first sound in TEA, TO, last sound in WALKED <t>, <d>, <th>
[θ]	last sound in BATH, WITH, the first sound in THISTLE <th> (voiceless), <t>
[ð]	first sound in THE, THIS, THAT, the last sound in BATHE <th> (voiced), <dh>
[ts]	<zz> in PIZZA <zz>, <ts>

4

[z]	last sound in IS, HAS, WAS, JAZZ, first sound in XYLEM <s>, <z>, <x>
[ʌ]	vowel in UP, SUN, WAS, LOVE <u>, <a>, <o>, <ou>, <oo>
[ʷʌ]	initial sound in ONE, ONCE <o>
[ə]	unstressed mid central vowel sound, first sound in ABOVE <a>, <e> <i> <o> <u> <y>, <ou>, <eau>
[u]	vowel in DO, MOVE, TOO, TUBE, BLEW, BRUISE <o>, <ou>, <oo>, <ew>, <oe>, <u>, <ui>, <eu>, <oeu>
[ju]	vowel sound in FEW, CUE, USE, DEUCE <u>, <ew>, <eu>, <eau>
[v]	first sound in VOTE, the last sound in OF <f>, <v>
[w]	first sound in WATER, WHAT <w>, <wh>, <u>
[wɑ]	<oi> in SOIREE <oi>
[j]	initial consonant in YAM, YES <y>, <i>, <j>
[ɾ]	middle sound in METAL, MEDAL <d>, <t>
[ʔ]	sound after the first <u> in UH-OH <h>

Other Phone Combinations

[əl]	last syllable in CRUMBLE, GRAVEL, DEVIL <le>, <el> <al> <il> <ul> <ol>
[əm]	last sound in PROBLEM, VENOM, JETSAM, DATUM , <om>, <am>, <um>
[ən]	last syllable in KITTEN <en>, <an> <on>
[ɑɹ]	last sound in CAR, STAR <ar>
[ɜɹ]	(stressed) the <Vr> sound in WERE, HER, FUR, FIR <er>, <ir>, <yr>, <or>, <ur>
[əɹ]	(unstressed) <Vr> sound in BAKER, LIAR, EDITOR, KEFIR, SULFUR <er>, <ar>, <or>, <yr>, <ir>, <ur>
[eɹ]	<Vr> sound in WHERE, WEAR, WARE <er> <ear> <ar>
[ɔɹ]	<Vr> sound in OR, ORE, OAR, FLOOR, FOUR, WAR <or>, <ar>, <oor>, <oar>, <our>
[ɑʊər]	<Vr> sound in OUR <our>
[jɜɹ]/[jəɹ]	<ur> sound in FURY, URANIUM <ur>
[ɪɹ]	<Vr> sound in SPIRIT, LYRIC <ir>, <yr>

This spelling program includes spellings of [ən], [əm], and [əl] because of the similarity to the syllabic [n̩], [m̩], and [l̩] and spellings of r-colored vowels.

List 1

Function words. <e> can spell [i]. A digraph is two letters that spell one sound.

a	an	I
the	be	me
he	she	we

(1) Read each spelling word. Write each word three times.

a The word *a* can be stressed [eɪ] or unstressed [ə].

_____   _____   _____

- - - - - - - - - -   - - - - - - - - - -   - - - - - - - - - -

_____   _____   _____

an The words *a*, *an*, and *one* all came from the Old English word *an* meaning "one."

_____   _____   _____

- - - - - - - - - -   - - - - - - - - - -   - - - - - - - - - -

_____   _____   _____

I The word *I* is always capitalized.

_____   _____   _____

- - - - - - - - - -   - - - - - - - - - -   - - - - - - - - - -

_____   _____   _____

the The word *the* can be stressed or unstressed. <th> is a digraph that spells [ð].

_____   _____   _____

- - - - - - - - - -   - - - - - - - - - -   - - - - - - - - - -

_____   _____   _____

be The word *be* is an irregular verb. Its forms are *am*, *is*, *are*, *was*, *were*, *been*, and *being*.

_____   _____   _____

- - - - - - - - - -   - - - - - - - - - -   - - - - - - - - - -

_____   _____   _____

me The word *me* is related to *my* an *mine*.

_____   _____   _____

- - - - - - - - - -   - - - - - - - - - -   - - - - - - - - - -

_____   _____   _____

he   The word *he* is related to *him* and *his*.

_____   _____   _____
- - - - - - - - - -   - - - - - - - - - -   - - - - - - - - - -
_____   _____   _____

she   <sh> is a digraph that spells [ʃ].

_____   _____   _____
- - - - - - - - - -   - - - - - - - - - -   - - - - - - - - - -
_____   _____   _____

we

_____   _____   _____
- - - - - - - - - -   - - - - - - - - - -   - - - - - - - - - -
_____   _____   _____

(2) Write the words in alphabetical (ABC) order.

a	an	be
he	I	me
she	the	we

_____   _____   _____
- - - - - - - - - -   - - - - - - - - - -   - - - - - - - - - -
_____   _____   _____

_____   _____   _____
- - - - - - - - - -   - - - - - - - - - -   - - - - - - - - - -
_____   _____   _____

_____   _____   _____
- - - - - - - - - -   - - - - - - - - - -   - - - - - - - - - -
_____   _____   _____

(3) Write the word(s) in the blanks. Read each sentence.

_____   _____

- - - - - - - - - - - -   - - - - - - - - - - - -

_____ am   _____ child.
I   a

_____   _____

- - - - - - - - - - - -   - - - - - - - - - - - -

_____ eat   _____ apple.
I   an

_____   _____

- - - - - - - - - - - -   - - - - - - - - - - - -

_____ is   _____ dog.
He   a

_____   _____

- - - - - - - - - - - -   - - - - - - - - - - - -

_____ is   _____ cat.
She   a

_____   _____

- - - - - - - - - - - -   - - - - - - - - - - - -

_____ see   _____ pig.
We   the

_____   _____

- - - - - - - - - - - -   - - - - - - - - - - - -

_____ sees _____ .
She   me

_____   _____

- - - - - - - - - - - -   - - - - - - - - - - - -

_____ feed _____ baby.
I   the

     _____   _____

     - - - - - - - - - -   - - - - - - - - - -

Don't _____ sad. _____ happy!
    be   Be

Did _____ eat _____ food?
he   the

Did _____ read _____ book?
she   the

_____ will _____ teacher.
I   be a

_____ will _____ baker.
He   be a

_____ will _____ farmer.
She   be a

_____ will _____ artists.
We   be

_____ man is _____ singer.
The   a

_____ woman is _____ actor.
The   an

10

(4) Write your own sentences using the spelling words.

(5) Listen to and write each spelling word.

_____   _____   _____
- - - - - - - - - - - -   - - - - - - - - - - - -   - - - - - - - - - - - -
_____   _____   _____

_____   _____   _____
- - - - - - - - - - - -   - - - - - - - - - - - -   - - - - - - - - - - - -
_____   _____   _____

_____   _____   _____
- - - - - - - - - - - -   - - - - - - - - - - - -   - - - - - - - - - - - -
_____   _____   _____

Review any words that you missed on the test.

_____   _____   _____
- - - - - - - - - - - -   - - - - - - - - - - - -   - - - - - - - - - - - -
_____   _____   _____

_____   _____   _____
- - - - - - - - - - - -   - - - - - - - - - - - -   - - - - - - - - - - - -
_____   _____   _____

_____   _____   _____
- - - - - - - - - - - -   - - - - - - - - - - - -   - - - - - - - - - - - -
_____   _____   _____

_____   _____   _____
- - - - - - - - - - - -   - - - - - - - - - - - -   - - - - - - - - - - - -
_____   _____   _____

_____   _____   _____
- - - - - - - - - - - -   - - - - - - - - - - - -   - - - - - - - - - - - -
_____   _____   _____

<i> can spell [ɪ].

it	its	it's	in
if	is	him	his

(1) Read each spelling word. Write each word three times.

it   The <i> spells [ɪ].

_____   _____   _____

- - - - - - - - - - - - - -   - - - - - - - - - - - - - -   - - - - - - - - - - - - - -

_____   _____   _____

its   The word *its* is a possessive pronoun and determiner that means "belonging to it."
<ts> spells a consonant cluster. <ɪt + s -> its>

_____   _____   _____

- - - - - - - - - - - - - -   - - - - - - - - - - - - - -   - - - - - - - - - - - - - -

_____   _____   _____

it's   The word *it's* is a contraction of *it is*.

_____   _____   _____

- - - - - - - - - - - - - -   - - - - - - - - - - - - - -   - - - - - - - - - - - - - -

_____   _____   _____

in

_____   _____   _____

- - - - - - - - - - - - - -   - - - - - - - - - - - - - -   - - - - - - - - - - - - - -

_____   _____   _____

if

_____   _____   _____

- - - - - - - - - - - - - -   - - - - - - - - - - - - - -   - - - - - - - - - - - - - -

_____   _____   _____

is   The <s> spells [z]. See also *his*.

_____   _____   _____

- - - - - - - - - - - - - -   - - - - - - - - - - - - - -   - - - - - - - - - - - - - -

_____   _____   _____

him
The word *him* is related to *he* and *his*.
The <m> in *him* is related to the <m> in *them* and *whom*.

---

his
The word *his* is related to *he* and *him*. The <s> spells [z]. See also *is*.

---

(2) Write the words in alphabetical (ABC) order.

him	his	if	in
is	it	it's	its

(3) Write the word(s) and/or sentences in the blanks. Read each sentence.

_____   _____

_____ am   _____ .
I   it

_____   _____

_____ see   _____ .
I   him

_____   _____

_____ sees   _____ .
He   him

_____

_____
He is it.

_____

_____
She is it.

_____

_____ cat.
It is a

_____

_____
It is his.

_____

_____ birthday.
It's his

_____   _____

_____ party _____ you come.
It's a   if

15

_____   _____
- - - - - - - - - - - - -   - - - - - - - - - - - - -
_____ cat hurt _____ paw.
The   its

_____   _____
- - - - - - - - - - - - -   - - - - - - - - - - - - -
_____ paw _____ hurt.
Its   is

_____   _____
- - - - - - - - - - - - -   - - - - - - - - - - - - -
_____ not _____ .
It is   his

_____
- -

His is in it.

_____
- -

It is in his.

_____
- -

She is in it.

_____
- -

It's his in it.

_____   _____
- - - - - - - - - - - - -   - - - - - - - - - - - - -
_____ not _____
It is   his in it.

_____
- -
Tell _____
him if it is his.

(4) Write your own sentences using the spelling words.

(5) Listen to and write each spelling word.

Review any words that you missed on the test.

List 3

<a> can spell [æ].

am	at	as
and	that	have
has	had	can

(1) Read each spelling word. Write each word three times.

am

_____   _____   _____
- - - - - - - - -   - - - - - - - - -   - - - - - - - - -
_____   _____   _____

at

_____   _____   _____
- - - - - - - - -   - - - - - - - - -   - - - - - - - - -
_____   _____   _____

as   The <s> spells [z]. See also *is* and *his*.

_____   _____   _____
- - - - - - - - -   - - - - - - - - -   - - - - - - - - -
_____   _____   _____

and   <nd> spells a consonant cluster.

_____   _____   _____
- - - - - - - - -   - - - - - - - - -   - - - - - - - - -
_____   _____   _____

that   <th> is a digraph that spells [ð].

_____   _____   _____
- - - - - - - - -   - - - - - - - - -   - - - - - - - - -
_____   _____   _____

have   The word *have* ends with a replaceable <e> to keep the word from ending with a <v>.

_____   _____   _____
- - - - - - - - -   - - - - - - - - -   - - - - - - - - -
_____   _____   _____

has   The <s> spells [z]. See also *as*.

_____   _____   _____
- - - - - - - - -   - - - - - - - - -   - - - - - - - - -
_____   _____   _____

had   The words *have*, *has*, and *had* are related.

_____   _____   _____
- - - - - - - - -   - - - - - - - - -   - - - - - - - - -
_____   _____   _____

can   <c> spells [k] before <a, o, u>. The word *can* is related to *could*.

_____   _____   _____
- - - - - - - - -   - - - - - - - - -   - - - - - - - - -
_____   _____   _____

(2) Write the words in alphabetical (ABC) order.

am	and	as
at	can	had
has	have	that

_____   _____   _____
- - - - - - - - -   - - - - - - - - -   - - - - - - - - -
_____   _____   _____

_____   _____   _____
- - - - - - - - -   - - - - - - - - -   - - - - - - - - -
_____   _____   _____

_____   _____   _____
- - - - - - - - -   - - - - - - - - -   - - - - - - - - -
_____   _____   _____

(3) Write the word(s) and/or sentences in the blanks. Read each sentence.

_____

- -

_____ home.

I am at

_____

- -

_____ said.

It's as he

_____   _____

- - - - - - - - - - - - - - - - - - -   - - - - - - - - - - -

_____ see _____

She and I   him.

_____   _____

- - - - - - - - - - - - - - - - - -   - - - - - - - - - - - -

_____ fast _____

I am as   as him.

_____   _____

- - - - - - - - - - - - - - - - - -   - - - - - - - - - - - -

_____ fun _____

It is as   as that.

_____

- -

I have a can.

_____

- -

He has a can.

_____

- -

She had a can.

_____

- -

Can I have that?

He can have that.

She can have that.

We can have that.

Can we have it?

We can have it.

That is it!

I have had it.

We have had it.

She has had it.

He has had it.

(4) Write your own sentences using the spelling words.

(5) Listen to and write each spelling word.

Review any words that you missed on the test.

List 4

<u> and <a> can spell [ʌ]. <o> can spell [ʌ] before <m>, <n>, <u>, and <v>.

us	up	but
was	what	come
some	done	none

(1) Read each spelling word. Write each word three times.

us   The word *us* is related to *our* and *ours*.

_____   _____   _____

- - - - - - - - - -   - - - - - - - - - -   - - - - - - - - - -

_____   _____   _____

up

_____   _____   _____

- - - - - - - - - -   - - - - - - - - - -   - - - - - - - - - -

_____   _____   _____

but

_____   _____   _____

- - - - - - - - - -   - - - - - - - - - -   - - - - - - - - - -

_____   _____   _____

was   The <s> spells [z]. See also *as* and *has*.

_____   _____   _____

- - - - - - - - - -   - - - - - - - - - -   - - - - - - - - - -

_____   _____   _____

what   <wh> is a digraph that spells [w]. Compare the question words *where*, *when*, *why*, and *which*.

_____   _____   _____

- - - - - - - - - -   - - - - - - - - - -   - - - - - - - - - -

_____   _____   _____

come   <c> spells [k] before <a, o, u>. <o> can spell [ʌ] before <m>, <n>, <u>, and <v>. The <e> is a replaceable <e>.

_____   _____   _____

- - - - - - - - - -   - - - - - - - - - -   - - - - - - - - - -

_____   _____   _____

some <o> can spell [ʌ] before <m>, <n>, <u>, and <v>.

_____   _____   _____

- - - - - - - - - -   - - - - - - - - - -   - - - - - - - - - -

_____   _____   _____

done <o> can spell [ʌ] before <m>, <n>, <u>, and <v>. <Do + ne -> done>
The word is the past participle of the verb *do*.

_____   _____   _____

- - - - - - - - - -   - - - - - - - - - -   - - - - - - - - - -

_____   _____   _____

none <o> can spell [ʌ] before <m>, <n>, <u>, and <v>. <n + One -> none>

_____   _____   _____

- - - - - - - - - -   - - - - - - - - - -   - - - - - - - - - -

_____   _____   _____

(2) Write the words in alphabetical (ABC) order.

but	come	done
none	some	up
us	was	what

_____   _____   _____

- - - - - - - - - -   - - - - - - - - - -   - - - - - - - - - -

_____   _____   _____

_____   _____   _____

- - - - - - - - - -   - - - - - - - - - -   - - - - - - - - - -

_____   _____   _____

_____   _____   _____

- - - - - - - - - -   - - - - - - - - - -   - - - - - - - - - -

_____   _____   _____

(3) Write the word(s) and/or sentences in the blanks. Read each sentence.

_____   _____

- - - - - - - - - - - - -   - - - - - - - - - - - -

_____ with _____ .

Come   me

_____   _____

- - - - - - - - - - - - -   - - - - - - - - - - - -

_____ with _____ .

Come   us

- -

It is up.

- -

His was up.

- -

What was that?

- -

It is done.

- -

It was done.

- -

What was done?

- -

Some is done.

Some was done.

Was some done?

I have none.

Some have none.

But I am done.

But she is done.

But he was done.

What was done?

But what was up?

But what is up?

(4) Write your own sentences using the spelling words.

(5) Listen to and write each spelling word.

Review any words that you missed on the test.

List 5

<o> can spell [oʊ] and [ɑ].

no	so	go	gone	on
not	pot	lot	got	hot

(1) Read each spelling word. Write each word three times.

no

_____   _____   _____
- - - - - - - - - - -   - - - - - - - - - - -   - - - - - - - - - - -
_____   _____   _____

so

_____   _____   _____
- - - - - - - - - - -   - - - - - - - - - - -   - - - - - - - - - - -
_____   _____   _____

go   The <o> spells [oʊ] in *go* and [ɑ] in *gone*. <o> is the only grapheme that works across the word family.

_____   _____   _____
- - - - - - - - - - -   - - - - - - - - - - -   - - - - - - - - - - -
_____   _____   _____

gone   <Go + ne -> gone> The words *go*, *goes*, and *gone* are related.

_____   _____   _____
- - - - - - - - - - -   - - - - - - - - - - -   - - - - - - - - - - -
_____   _____   _____

on

_____   _____   _____
- - - - - - - - - - -   - - - - - - - - - - -   - - - - - - - - - - -
_____   _____   _____

not

_____   _____   _____
- - - - - - - - - - -   - - - - - - - - - - -   - - - - - - - - - - -
_____   _____   _____

pot

_____   _____   _____
- - - - - - - - - - -   - - - - - - - - - - -   - - - - - - - - - - -
_____   _____   _____

lot

got   The word *got* is the simple past of the verb *get*.

hot

(2) Write the words in alphabetical (ABC) order.

go	gone	got	hot	lot
no	not	on	pot	so

(3) Write the word(s) and/or sentences in the blanks. Read each sentence.

_____

- -
_____ fast.

He can go so

_____

- -
_____ slow.

She can go so

_____

- -

The pot is hot.

_____

- -

The pot is not hot.

_____

- -

I got a lot.

_____

- -

I got a pot.

_____

- -

I am not done.

_____

- -

He is not done.

_____

- -

She was not done.

I am not gone.

He is not gone.

She was not gone.

No! The pot is gone.

I have no pot.

Can we go?

We can go on up.

Come on in!

Go on up!

So it is on?

(4) Write your own sentences using the spelling words.

(5) Listen to and write each spelling word.

Review any words that you missed on the test.

List 6

<ar> can spell [ɑɹ]. <er> can spell [ɜɹ].

are	car	bar	jar
far	were	her	hers

(1) Read each spelling word. Write each word three times.

are   The replaceable <e> marks the lexical spelling.

_____   _____   _____

- - - - - - - - - -   - - - - - - - - - -   - - - - - - - - - -

_____   _____   _____

car   <c> spells [k] before <a, o, u>.

_____   _____   _____

- - - - - - - - - -   - - - - - - - - - -   - - - - - - - - - -

_____   _____   _____

bar

_____   _____   _____

- - - - - - - - - -   - - - - - - - - - -   - - - - - - - - - -

_____   _____   _____

jar

_____   _____   _____

- - - - - - - - - -   - - - - - - - - - -   - - - - - - - - - -

_____   _____   _____

far

_____   _____   _____

- - - - - - - - - -   - - - - - - - - - -   - - - - - - - - - -

_____   _____   _____

were The replaceable <e> marks the lexical spelling.

_____ _____ _____
- - - - - - - - - - - - - - - - - - - - - - - - - - - - - - - - - - - - - - -
_____ _____ _____

her

_____ _____ _____
- - - - - - - - - - - - - - - - - - - - - - - - - - - - - - - - - - - - - - -
_____ _____ _____

hers The <s> spells [z]. See also _is_, _was_, _as_, _has_, and _his_. <Her + s -> hers>

_____ _____ _____
- - - - - - - - - - - - - - - - - - - - - - - - - - - - - - - - - - - - - - -
_____ _____ _____

(2) Write the words in alphabetical (ABC) order.

are	bar	car	far
her	hers	jar	were

_____ _____ _____
- - - - - - - - - - - - - - - - - - - - - - - - - - - - - - - - - - - - - - -
_____ _____ _____

_____ _____ _____
- - - - - - - - - - - - - - - - - - - - - - - - - - - - - - - - - - - - - - -
_____ _____ _____

_____ _____
- - - - - - - - - - - - - - - - - - - - - - - - - -
_____ _____

38

(3) Write the word(s) and/or sentences in the blanks. Read each sentence.

_____

- -
_____ here.

Her car is

_____

- -
_____ full.

The jar is

_____

- -
_____ chocolate.

The bar is

_____

- -

The car is hers.

_____

- -

The jar is hers.

_____

- -

The bar is hers.

_____

- -

The bar and jar are hers.

_____

- -

_____

- -

Her car is gone.

We are gone.

We are not gone.

We were gone.

We were not gone.

Are we gone?

Were we gone?

We go far.

We have gone far.

She has gone far.

He has gone far.

(4) Write your own sentences using the spelling words.

(5) Listen to and write each spelling word.

Review any words that you missed on the test.

<o>, <oo>, and <ou> can spell [u].

do	to	too	two
who	you	your	yours

(1) Read each spelling word. Write each word three times.

do

_____   _____   _____

- - - - - - - - - -   - - - - - - - - - -   - - - - - - - - - -

_____   _____   _____

to

Both *to* and *too* came from the Old English word *to*. *To* can be stressed [u] or unstressed [ə].

_____   _____   _____

- - - - - - - - - -   - - - - - - - - - -   - - - - - - - - - -

_____   _____   _____

too

The <oo> digraph distinguishes adverb *too* from preposition/p-word *to*.

_____   _____   _____

- - - - - - - - - -   - - - - - - - - - -   - - - - - - - - - -

_____   _____   _____

two

The <w> in the number *two* marks a relationship with related words like *twelve*, *twenty*, *twin*, and *twice*.

_____   _____   _____

- - - - - - - - - -   - - - - - - - - - -   - - - - - - - - - -

_____   _____   _____

who

The digraph <wh> can spell [h] before <o> like in *whom*, *whose*, and *whole*.

_____   _____   _____

- - - - - - - - - -   - - - - - - - - - -   - - - - - - - - - -

_____   _____   _____

you   The word *you* can end with a <u> because the pronoun *you* is a function word.

_____   _____   _____

- - - - - - - - - - - -   - - - - - - - - - - - -   - - - - - - - - - - - -

_____   _____   _____

your   The <ou> in *your* and *your* marks the relationship with the pronoun *you*.

_____   _____   _____

- - - - - - - - - - - -   - - - - - - - - - - - -   - - - - - - - - - - - -

_____   _____   _____

yours <Your + s -> yours>

_____   _____   _____

- - - - - - - - - - - -   - - - - - - - - - - - -   - - - - - - - - - - - -

_____   _____   _____

(2) Write the words in alphabetical (ABC) order.

do	to	too	two
who	you	your	yours

_____   _____   _____

- - - - - - - - - - - -   - - - - - - - - - - - -   - - - - - - - - - - - -

_____   _____   _____

_____   _____   _____

- - - - - - - - - - - -   - - - - - - - - - - - -   - - - - - - - - - - - -

_____   _____   _____

_____   _____

- - - - - - - - - - - -   - - - - - - - - - - - -

_____   _____

(3) Write the word(s) and/or sentences in the blanks. Read each sentence.

_____

- -
_____ fast.

Your car is

_____

- -
_____ slow.

Your car is not

_____

- -

The car is yours.

_____

- -

Who are you?

_____

- -

Who were you?

_____

- -

You go too.

_____

- -

Two are gone.

_____

- -

Two have come.

_____

- -

What are you?

What were you?

Yours was what?

What was yours?

You two are on.

The pot is yours.

Your pot is hot!

No, two are hot!

Your car is far.

Yours is far too!

Yours is too far.

(4) Write your own sentences using the spelling words.

(5) Listen to and write each spelling word.

Review any words that you missed on the test.

List 8

<o> can spell [$^{w}ʌ$]. <y> can spell [aɪ].

one	once	by
my	why	shy
cry	try	dry

(1) Read each spelling word. Write each word three times.

one   The <o> in *one* and *once* spells [$^{w}ʌ$]. The word *one* is related to *a* and *an*.

_____ _____ _____

- - - - - - - - - - - - - - - - - - - - - - - - - - - - - -

_____ _____ _____

once   *Once* is related to *one*. <c> spells [s] before <e, i, y>.

_____ _____ _____

- - - - - - - - - - - - - - - - - - - - - - - - - - - - - -

_____ _____ _____

by

_____ _____ _____

- - - - - - - - - - - - - - - - - - - - - - - - - - - - - -

_____ _____ _____

my   The word *my* is related to *me* and *mine*.

_____ _____ _____

- - - - - - - - - - - - - - - - - - - - - - - - - - - - - -

_____ _____ _____

why   <wh> is a digraph that spells [w]. Compare the question words *what*, *where*, *when*, and *which*.

_____ _____ _____

- - - - - - - - - - - - - - - - - - - - - - - - - - - - - -

_____ _____ _____

shy   <sh> is a digraph that spells [ʃ].

_____ _____ _____

- - - - - - - - - - - - - - - - - - - - - - - - - - - - - -

_____ _____ _____

cry   <cr> spells a consonant cluster.

_____   _____   _____
- - - - - - - -   - - - - - - - -   - - - - - - - -
_____   _____   _____

try   The [tɹ] consonant cluster sounds similar to [t͡ʃɹ] because of the position of the tongue in the mouth for [t] and [ɹ].

_____   _____   _____
- - - - - - - -   - - - - - - - -   - - - - - - - -
_____   _____   _____

dry   The <dr> consonant cluster sounds like [d͡ʒɹ] because of the position of the tongue in the mouth for [d] and [ɹ].

_____   _____   _____
- - - - - - - -   - - - - - - - -   - - - - - - - -
_____   _____   _____

(2) Write the words in alphabetical (ABC) order.

by	cry	dry
my	once	one
shy	try	why

_____   _____   _____
- - - - - - - -   - - - - - - - -   - - - - - - - -
_____   _____   _____

_____   _____   _____
- - - - - - - -   - - - - - - - -   - - - - - - - -
_____   _____   _____

_____   _____   _____
- - - - - - - -   - - - - - - - -   - - - - - - - -
_____   _____   _____

(3) Write the sentences on the lines. Read each sentence.

I can try it.

You can try it.

We can try once.

I have one.

Do you have one?

I had one once.

Once I had one.

Why do you cry?

Why do you try?

Why are you shy?

I am shy.

We are shy.

She is shy too.

He was shy once.

It is dry.

Is one dry?

I am by my car.

My car is dry.

I try my car.

(4) Write your own sentences using the spelling words.

(5) Listen to and write each spelling word.

Review any words that you missed on the test.

List 9

<o> can spell [ʌ] before <m>, <n>, <u>, and <v>. <o> can spell [ɔ].

of	off	from
come	some	love
or	for	nor

(1) Read each spelling word. Write each word three times.

of

The <o> spells [ʌ]. The <f> spells [v].

_____ _____ _____

- - - - - - - - - - - - - - - - - - - - - - - - - - - - - -

_____ _____ _____

off

The spelling of *off* links the word to *of*. Both *of* and *off* came from Old English *of*.

_____ _____ _____

- - - - - - - - - - - - - - - - - - - - - - - - - - - - - -

_____ _____ _____

from

<o> can spell [ʌ] before <m>, <n>, <u>, and <v>. <fr> spells a consonant cluster.

_____ _____ _____

- - - - - - - - - - - - - - - - - - - - - - - - - - - - - -

_____ _____ _____

come

<c> spells [k] before <a, o, u>. <o> can spell [ʌ] before <m>, <n>, <u>, and <v>. The <e> is a replaceable <e>.

_____ _____ _____

- - - - - - - - - - - - - - - - - - - - - - - - - - - - - -

_____ _____ _____

some

<o> can spell [ʌ] before <m>, <n>, <u>, and <v>.

_____ _____ _____

- - - - - - - - - - - - - - - - - - - - - - - - - - - - - -

_____ _____ _____

love

<o> can spell [ʌ] before <m>, <n>, <u>, and <v>.
The replaceable <e> keeps the word from ending in <v>.

_____ _____ _____

- - - - - - - - - - - - - - - - - - - - - - - - - - - - - -

_____ _____ _____

or   The word *or* is a function word.

_____   _____   _____

- - - - - - - - - -   - - - - - - - - - -   - - - - - - - - - -

_____   _____   _____

for   The word *for* is a function word.

_____   _____   _____

- - - - - - - - - -   - - - - - - - - - -   - - - - - - - - - -

_____   _____   _____

nor   The word *nor* is a function word. <n + Or -> nor>

_____   _____   _____

- - - - - - - - - -   - - - - - - - - - -   - - - - - - - - - -

_____   _____   _____

(2) Write the words in alphabetical (ABC) order.

come	for	from
love	nor	of
off	or	some

_____   _____   _____

- - - - - - - - - -   - - - - - - - - - -   - - - - - - - - - -

_____   _____   _____

_____   _____   _____

- - - - - - - - - -   - - - - - - - - - -   - - - - - - - - - -

_____   _____   _____

(3) Write the sentences on the lines. Read each sentence.

_____

- -

_____

I love it.

_____

- -

_____

Do you love it?

_____

- -

_____

Nor do we love it.

_____

- -

_____

Come off of it.

_____

- -

_____

He or she can come.

_____

- -

_____

Some of it is.

_____

- -

_____

Some of it is not.

_____

- -

_____

Come for some.

_____

- -

_____

It is from you.

It is from him or her.

It is not from us or me.

Nor is it from you or me.

Some is from me.

Some is for you.

Some of it is for you and me.

(4) Write your own sentences using the spelling words.

(5) Listen to and write each spelling word.

Review any words that you missed on the test.

<i> can spell [ɪ].

with	this	bit
fit	sit	hit
pit	lit	kit

(1) Read each spelling word. Write each word three times.

with <th> is a digraph that spells [ð].

_____ _____ _____
- - - - - - - - - - - - - - - - - - - - - - - - - - -
_____ _____ _____

this <th> is a digraph that spells [ð].

_____ _____ _____
- - - - - - - - - - - - - - - - - - - - - - - - - - -
_____ _____ _____

bit The word *bit* is the simple past of the verb *bite*.

_____ _____ _____
- - - - - - - - - - - - - - - - - - - - - - - - - - -
_____ _____ _____

fit

_____ _____ _____
- - - - - - - - - - - - - - - - - - - - - - - - - - -
_____ _____ _____

sit

_____ _____ _____
- - - - - - - - - - - - - - - - - - - - - - - - - - -
_____ _____ _____

hit

_____ _____ _____
- - - - - - - - - - - - - - - - - - - - - - - - - - -
_____ _____ _____

pit

_____ _____ _____
- - - - - - - - - - - - - - - - - - - - - - - - - - -
_____ _____ _____

lit   The word *lit* is the simple past of the verb *light*.

_____ _____ _____
- - - - - - - - - - - - - - - - - - - - - - - - - - -
_____ _____ _____

kit

_____ _____ _____
- - - - - - - - - - - - - - - - - - - - - - - - - - -
_____ _____ _____

(2) Write the words in alphabetical (ABC) order.

bit	fit	hit
kit	lit	pit
sit	this	with

_____ _____ _____
- - - - - - - - - - - - - - - - - - - - - - - - - - -
_____ _____ _____

_____ _____ _____
- - - - - - - - - - - - - - - - - - - - - - - - - - -
_____ _____ _____

(3) Write the sentences on the lines. Read each sentence.

_____

- -

Sit with me.

_____

- -

It can sit.

_____

- -

Come with us.

_____

- -

I bit this.

_____

- -

She bit this.

_____

- -

He bit this.

_____

- -

I fit in this.

_____

- -

I hit it.

_____

- -

Hit it with this.

I lit this.

I lit it.

It is lit.

This is lit.

The kit bit it.

The kit bit this.

It is in a pit.

I am in a pit.

The kit is in a pit with this one.

(4) Write your own sentences using the spelling words.

(5) Listen to and write each spelling word.

_____   _____   _____
- - - - - - - - - - - - - - -   - - - - - - - - - - - - - - -   - - - - - - - - - - - - - - -
_____   _____   _____

_____   _____   _____
- - - - - - - - - - - - - - -   - - - - - - - - - - - - - - -   - - - - - - - - - - - - - - -
_____   _____   _____

_____   _____   _____
- - - - - - - - - - - - - - -   - - - - - - - - - - - - - - -   - - - - - - - - - - - - - - -
_____   _____   _____

Review any words that you missed on the test.

_____   _____   _____
- - - - - - - - - - - - - - -   - - - - - - - - - - - - - - -   - - - - - - - - - - - - - - -
_____   _____   _____

_____   _____   _____
- - - - - - - - - - - - - - -   - - - - - - - - - - - - - - -   - - - - - - - - - - - - - - -
_____   _____   _____

_____   _____   _____
- - - - - - - - - - - - - - -   - - - - - - - - - - - - - - -   - - - - - - - - - - - - - - -
_____   _____   _____

_____   _____   _____
- - - - - - - - - - - - - - -   - - - - - - - - - - - - - - -   - - - - - - - - - - - - - - -
_____   _____   _____

_____   _____   _____
- - - - - - - - - - - - - - -   - - - - - - - - - - - - - - -   - - - - - - - - - - - - - - -
_____   _____   _____

List 11

<i> can spell [ɪ]. <a> can spell [ɔ]. <ll> spells [l]. <l> can mark <a> as spelling [ɔ].

will	ill	still
all	ball	call
fall	hall	tall

(1) Read each spelling word. Write each word three times.

will   The <ll> marks a lexical spelling. The word *will* is related to *would*.

_____   _____   _____

- - - - - - - - - - - - -   - - - - - - - - - - - - -   - - - - - - - - - - - - -

_____   _____   _____

ill

_____   _____   _____

- - - - - - - - - - - - -   - - - - - - - - - - - - -   - - - - - - - - - - - - -

_____   _____   _____

still   <st> spells a consonant cluster.

_____   _____   _____

- - - - - - - - - - - - -   - - - - - - - - - - - - -   - - - - - - - - - - - - -

_____   _____   _____

all   The <l> marks the <a> as spelling [ɔ].

_____   _____   _____

- - - - - - - - - - - - -   - - - - - - - - - - - - -   - - - - - - - - - - - - -

_____   _____   _____

ball

_____   _____   _____

- - - - - - - - - - - - -   - - - - - - - - - - - - -   - - - - - - - - - - - - -

_____   _____   _____

call   <c> spells [k] before <a, o, u>.

_____   _____   _____

- - - - - - - - - - - - -   - - - - - - - - - - - - -   - - - - - - - - - - - - -

_____   _____   _____

fall

_____

- - - - - - - - - - - -

_____

hall

_____

- - - - - - - - - - - -

_____

tall

_____

- - - - - - - - - - - -

_____

(2) Write the words in alphabetical (ABC) order.

all	ball	call
fall	hall	ill
still	tall	will

_____

- - - - - - - - - - - -

_____

_____

- - - - - - - - - - - -

_____

(3) Write the sentences on the lines. Read each sentence.

_____

- -

Will we fall?

_____

- -

We will fall.

_____

- -

Will he call?

_____

- -

He will call.

_____

- -

I am tall.

_____

- -

You are tall.

_____

- -

She is tall.

_____

- -

I have a ball.

_____

- -

The ball will fall.

I am ill.

I am still ill.

Are you ill too?

We all are ill.

I am in the hall.

It is in the hall.

The ball is in the hall still.

I fall on the ball in the hall.

(4) Write your own sentences using the spelling words.

(5) Listen to and write each spelling word.

Review any words that you missed on the test.

List 12

They, *them*, *their*, and *theirs*. <e> can spell [ɛ].

they	them	their	theirs	get
let	jet	pet	wet	met

(1) Read each spelling word. Write each word three times.

they   <th> is a digraph that spells [ð]. <ey> is a digraph that spells [eɪ].

_____   _____   _____

- - - - - - - - -   - - - - - - - - -   - - - - - - - - -

_____   _____   _____

them   <th> is a digraph that spells [ð]. <e> in *they*, *them*, *their*, and *theirs* links the related words.

_____   _____   _____

- - - - - - - - -   - - - - - - - - -   - - - - - - - - -

_____   _____   _____

their   <th> is a digraph that spells [ð].

_____   _____   _____

- - - - - - - - -   - - - - - - - - -   - - - - - - - - -

_____   _____   _____

theirs   <th> is a digraph that spells [ð]. <Their + s -> theirs> <s> spells [z].

_____   _____   _____

- - - - - - - - -   - - - - - - - - -   - - - - - - - - -

_____   _____   _____

get   The word *get* is related to *got*.

_____   _____   _____

- - - - - - - - -   - - - - - - - - -   - - - - - - - - -

_____   _____   _____

let

_____   _____   _____

- - - - - - - - -   - - - - - - - - -   - - - - - - - - -

jet

_____   _____   _____

- - - - - - - - -   - - - - - - - - -   - - - - - - - - -

_____   _____   _____

pet

wet

met   The word *met* is the simple past of the verb *meet*.

(2) Write the words in alphabetical (ABC) order.

get	jet	let	met	pet
their	theirs	them	they	wet

(3) Write the sentences on the lines. Read each sentence.

They get wet.

I get them wet.

Their pet is wet.

Theirs is wet.

Get the jet wet.

I met their pet.

Their pet met me.

Get their pet wet.

Get theirs wet.

We met them.

Get them wet.

Let them get wet.

They get their pet.

They get theirs wet.

Let me get wet.

They have met the wet pet.

They let their pet get the jet wet.

(4) Write your own sentences using the spelling words.

(5) Listen to and write each spelling word.

_____
- - - - - - - - - - - -
_____

_____
- - - - - - - - - - - -
_____

_____
- - - - - - - - - - - -
_____

_____
- - - - - - - - - - - -
_____

_____
- - - - - - - - - - - -
_____

_____
- - - - - - - - - - - -
_____

_____
- - - - - - - - - - - -
_____

Review any words that you missed on the test.

_____
- - - - - - - - - - - -
_____

_____
- - - - - - - - - - - -
_____

_____
- - - - - - - - - - - -
_____

_____
- - - - - - - - - - - -
_____

_____
- - - - - - - - - - - -
_____

_____
- - - - - - - - - - - -
_____

_____
- - - - - - - - - - - -
_____

_____
- - - - - - - - - - - -
_____

_____
- - - - - - - - - - - -
_____

List 13

<ay> can spell [eɪ].

say	may	way
day	pay	bay
stay	play	gray

(1) Read each spelling word. Write each word three times.

say   The word is related to *says* and *said*.

_____   _____   _____

- - - - - - - - - - -   - - - - - - - - - - -   - - - - - - - - - - -

_____   _____   _____

may   The word *may* is related to *might*.

_____   _____   _____

- - - - - - - - - - -   - - - - - - - - - - -   - - - - - - - - - - -

_____   _____   _____

way

_____   _____   _____

- - - - - - - - - - -   - - - - - - - - - - -   - - - - - - - - - - -

_____   _____   _____

day

_____   _____   _____

- - - - - - - - - - -   - - - - - - - - - - -   - - - - - - - - - - -

_____   _____   _____

pay

_____   _____   _____

- - - - - - - - - - -   - - - - - - - - - - -   - - - - - - - - - - -

_____   _____   _____

bay

_____   _____   _____

- - - - - - - - - - -   - - - - - - - - - - -   - - - - - - - - - - -

_____   _____   _____

stay   <st> spells a consonant cluster.

_____   _____   _____

- - - - - - - - - - - -   - - - - - - - - - - - -   - - - - - - - - - - - -

_____   _____   _____

play   <pl> spells a consonant cluster.

_____   _____   _____

- - - - - - - - - - - -   - - - - - - - - - - - -   - - - - - - - - - - - -

_____   _____   _____

gray   <gr> spells a consonant cluster.

_____   _____   _____

- - - - - - - - - - - -   - - - - - - - - - - - -   - - - - - - - - - - - -

_____   _____   _____

(2) Write the words in alphabetical (ABC) order.

bay	day	gray
may	pay	play
say	stay	way

_____   _____   _____

- - - - - - - - - - - -   - - - - - - - - - - - -   - - - - - - - - - - - -

_____   _____   _____

_____   _____   _____

- - - - - - - - - - - -   - - - - - - - - - - - -   - - - - - - - - - - - -

_____   _____   _____

(3) Write the sentences on the lines. Read each sentence.

_____

- -
_____

They may pay.

_____

- -
_____

They may say no.

_____

- -
_____

They do say no.

_____

- -
_____

They may play.

_____

- -
_____

They may not play.

_____

- -
_____

They may stay.

_____

- -
_____

They may not stay.

_____

- -
_____

The day is gray.

_____

- -
_____

I go to the bay.

The bay is gray.

I go this way.

I go that way.

Stay with me.

We may stay.

We may not stay.

May we stay?

May we play?

We say we may stay at the bay.

(4) Write your own sentences using the spelling words.

(5) Listen to and write each spelling word.

Review any words that you missed on the test.

List 14

Here, there, and *where.* <ee> can spell [i].

here	there	where	see
bee	free	tree	three

(1) Read each spelling word. Write each word three times.

here

The final <e> marks the first <e> as spelling [i].
The words *here, there,* and *where* all share the letters <here>.

_____ _____ _____

- - - - - - - - - - - - - - - - - - - - - - - - - - - - - -

_____ _____ _____

there

<th> is a digraph that spells [ð]. The <er> spells [eɹ]. The final <e> is a marker.

_____ _____ _____

- - - - - - - - - - - - - - - - - - - - - - - - - - - - - -

_____ _____ _____

where

<wh> is a digraph that spells [w]. Compare the question words *what, when, why,* and *which.*
The <er> spells [eɹ]. The final <e> is a marker.

_____ _____ _____

- - - - - - - - - - - - - - - - - - - - - - - - - - - - - -

_____ _____ _____

see

<ee> is a digraph that spells [i].

_____ _____ _____

- - - - - - - - - - - - - - - - - - - - - - - - - - - - - -

_____ _____ _____

bee

_____ _____ _____

- - - - - - - - - - - - - - - - - - - - - - - - - - - - - -

_____ _____ _____

free

<fr> spells a consonant cluster.

_____ _____ _____

- - - - - - - - - - - - - - - - - - - - - - - - - - - - - -

_____ _____ _____

tree   The [tɹ] consonant cluster sounds similar to [t͡ʃɹ] because of the position of the tongue in the mouth for [t] and [ɹ].

_____   _____   _____

- - - - - - - - - - - -   - - - - - - - - - - - - -   - - - - - - - - - - - -

_____   _____   _____

three   <th> is a digraph that spells [θ]. <thr> spells a consonant cluster.

_____   _____   _____

- - - - - - - - - - - -   - - - - - - - - - - - - -   - - - - - - - - - - - -

_____   _____   _____

(2) Write the words in alphabetical (ABC) order.

bee	free	here	see
there	three	tree	where

_____   _____   _____

- - - - - - - - - - - -   - - - - - - - - - - - - -   - - - - - - - - - - - -

_____   _____   _____

_____   _____   _____

- - - - - - - - - - - -   - - - - - - - - - - - - -   - - - - - - - - - - - -

_____   _____   _____

_____   _____

- - - - - - - - - - - -   - - - - - - - - - - - - -

_____   _____

(3) Write the sentences on the lines. Read each sentence.

_____

I see a bee.

_____

They see a bee.

_____

The bee is free.

_____

We see a tree.

_____

They see three.

_____

Three are here.

_____

Three are there.

_____

Where are they?

_____

Where are the three?

A tree is here.

A tree is there.

Where is the tree?

I am free.

We are free.

You are free.

They are free.

It is free to see.

One bee is still here in a tall tree.

(4) Write your own sentences using the spelling words.

(5) Listen to and write each spelling word.

Review any words that you missed on the test.

List 15

Replaceable <e> can mark <i> as spelling [ɑɪ].

ride	life	bike	like	time
line	mine	fine	nine	five

(1) Read each spelling word. Write each word three times.

ride

life

bike

like

time

line

mine   The word *mine* is related to *me* and *my*.

fine

_____

- - - - - - - -

_____

nine

_____

- - - - - - - -

_____

five

_____

- - - - - - - -

_____

(2) Write the words in alphabetical (ABC) order.

bike	fine	five	life	like
line	mine	nine	ride	time

(3) Write the sentences on the lines. Read each sentence.

_____

- -

_____

I am fine.

_____

- -

_____

I am five.

_____

- -

_____

I am nine.

_____

- -

_____

They are nine.

_____

- -

_____

Nine were in line.

_____

- -

_____

Five were in line.

_____

- -

_____

I ride a bike.

_____

- -

_____

I like the bike.

_____

- -

_____

Mine is fine.

Mine is on time.

I like my life.

The time is five.

The time is nine.

I like to ride.

They like to ride.

They like to ride the fine bike.

Mine like to ride the fine bike.

(4) Write your own sentences using the spelling words.

(5) Listen to and write each spelling word.

_____

- - - - - - - - - - - -

_____

_____

- - - - - - - - - - - -

_____

_____

- - - - - - - - - - - -

_____

_____

- - - - - - - - - - - -

_____

Review any words that you missed on the test.

96

List 16

<ou> can spell [aʊ].

out	about	loud
cloud	found	sound
our	ours	hour

(1) Read each spelling word. Write each word three times.

out

_____ _____ _____
- - - - - - - - - - - - - - - - - - - - - - - -
_____ _____ _____

about   The <a> in *about* spells the unstressed [ə].

_____ _____ _____
- - - - - - - - - - - - - - - - - - - - - - - -
_____ _____ _____

loud

_____ _____ _____
- - - - - - - - - - - - - - - - - - - - - - - -
_____ _____ _____

cloud   <cl> spells a consonant cluster.

_____ _____ _____
- - - - - - - - - - - - - - - - - - - - - - - -
_____ _____ _____

found   <nd> spells a consonant cluster. The word is the simple past and past participle of the verb *find*.

_____ _____ _____
- - - - - - - - - - - - - - - - - - - - - - - -
_____ _____ _____

sound

_____ _____ _____
- - - - - - - - - - - - - - - - - - - - - - - -
_____ _____ _____

our   The word *our* can spell [aʊər] or [aɹ]. The <u> marks a relationship with the <u> in the word *us*.

_____   _____   _____
- - - - - - - - - -   - - - - - - - - - -   - - - - - - - - - -
_____   _____   _____

ours   <Our + s -> ours> <s> spells [z].

_____   _____   _____
- - - - - - - - - -   - - - - - - - - - -   - - - - - - - - - -
_____   _____   _____

hour   The <h> in *hour* distinguishes the word from the homophone *our*. The <h> also marks a relationship to related words such as *horology*, *horoscope*, and *horometer*.

_____   _____   _____
- - - - - - - - - -   - - - - - - - - - -   - - - - - - - - - -
_____   _____   _____

(2) Write the words in alphabetical (ABC) order.

about	cloud	found
hour	loud	our
ours	out	sound

_____   _____   _____
- - - - - - - - - -   - - - - - - - - - -   - - - - - - - - - -
_____   _____   _____

_____   _____   _____
- - - - - - - - - -   - - - - - - - - - -   - - - - - - - - - -
_____   _____   _____

_____   _____   _____
- - - - - - - - - -   - - - - - - - - - -   - - - - - - - - - -
_____   _____   _____

(3) Write the sentences on the lines. Read each sentence.

They are loud.

I am loud too.

The sound is loud.

I found a cloud.

The cloud is loud.

Our cloud is loud.

Ours is loud.

A book is about the loud cloud.

We found the book.

I go in an hour.

We go in an hour.

One hour has gone.

Ours is out and about.

Ours are out and about.

I found out.

We found out.

They found out.

We found them.

(4) Write your own sentences using the spelling words.

(5) Listen to and write each spelling word.

Review any words that you missed on the test.

List 17

Says and *said*. <e> can spell [ɛ].

says	said	when	then	well
red	bed	set	yes	went

(1) Read each spelling word. Write each word three times.

says The digraph <ay> can spell [ɛ] when reduced from [eɪ] in a word like *says*. <s> spells [z].
The words *says* and *said* are related to the verb *say*.

_____   _____   _____

- - - - - - - - -   - - - - - - - - -   - - - - - - - - -

_____   _____   _____

said The digraph <ai> can spell [ɛ] when reduced from [eɪ] in a word like *said*.

_____   _____   _____

- - - - - - - - -   - - - - - - - - -   - - - - - - - - -

_____   _____   _____

when <wh> is a digraph that spells [w]. Compare the question words *what*, *where*, *why*, and *which*.

_____   _____   _____

- - - - - - - - -   - - - - - - - - -   - - - - - - - - -

_____   _____   _____

then <th> is a digraph that spells [ð].

_____   _____   _____

- - - - - - - - -   - - - - - - - - -   - - - - - - - - -

_____   _____   _____

well <ll> is a digraph that marks the lexical spelling.

_____   _____   _____

- - - - - - - - -   - - - - - - - - -   - - - - - - - - -

_____   _____   _____

red

_____   _____   _____

- - - - - - - - -   - - - - - - - - -   - - - - - - - - -

_____   _____   _____

bed

_____   _____   _____
- - - - - - - - - - -   - - - - - - - - - - -   - - - - - - - - - - -
_____   _____   _____

set

_____   _____   _____
- - - - - - - - - - -   - - - - - - - - - - -   - - - - - - - - - - -
_____   _____   _____

yes

_____   _____   _____
- - - - - - - - - - -   - - - - - - - - - - -   - - - - - - - - - - -
_____   _____   _____

went   <nt> spells a consonant cluster.

_____   _____   _____
- - - - - - - - - - -   - - - - - - - - - - -   - - - - - - - - - - -
_____   _____   _____

(2) Write the words in alphabetical (ABC) order.

bed	red	said	says	set
then	well	went	when	yes

_____   _____   _____
- - - - - - - - - - -   - - - - - - - - - - -   - - - - - - - - - - -
_____   _____   _____

_____   _____   _____
- - - - - - - - - - -   - - - - - - - - - - -   - - - - - - - - - - -
_____   _____   _____

_____   _____   _____
- - - - - - - - - - -   - - - - - - - - - - -   - - - - - - - - - - -
_____   _____   _____

_____
- - - - - - - - - - -
_____

(3) Write the sentences on the lines. Read each sentence.

_____

- -

_____

I am well.

_____

- -

_____

I went to bed.

_____

- -

_____

My bed is red.

_____

- -

_____

He says yes.

_____

- -

_____

She says yes.

_____

- -

_____

They said yes.

_____

- -

_____

We said yes.

_____

- -

_____

You went when?

_____

- -

_____

When do you go?

It went well.

Then it went well.

The well is where?

Set it on the red bed.

You set it where?

I set it there.

They set is here.

We set it up.

Then he set it up.

She set it up then.

(4) Write your own sentences using the spelling words.

(5) Listen to and write each spelling word.

Review any words that you missed on the test.

List 18

<oo> and <u> can spell [ʊ].

book	cook	look
took	foot	good
wood	stood	put

(1) Read each spelling word. Write each word three times.

book

_____   _____   _____

- - - - - - - - - -   - - - - - - - - - -   - - - - - - - - - -

_____   _____   _____

cook <c> spells [k] before <a, o, u>.

_____   _____   _____

- - - - - - - - - -   - - - - - - - - - -   - - - - - - - - - -

_____   _____   _____

look

_____   _____   _____

- - - - - - - - - -   - - - - - - - - - -   - - - - - - - - - -

_____   _____   _____

took The word *took* is the simple past of the verb *take*.

_____   _____   _____

- - - - - - - - - -   - - - - - - - - - -   - - - - - - - - - -

_____   _____   _____

foot The word *foot* is related to the plural noun *feet*.

_____   _____   _____

- - - - - - - - - -   - - - - - - - - - -   - - - - - - - - - -

_____   _____   _____

good

_____   _____   _____

- - - - - - - - - -   - - - - - - - - - -   - - - - - - - - - -

_____   _____   _____

wood

_____   _____   _____
- - - - - - - - -   - - - - - - - - -   - - - - - - - - -
_____   _____   _____

stood   The word *stood* is the simple past and past participle of the verb *stand*.

_____   _____   _____
- - - - - - - - -   - - - - - - - - -   - - - - - - - - -
_____   _____   _____

put

_____   _____   _____
- - - - - - - - -   - - - - - - - - -   - - - - - - - - -
_____   _____   _____

(2) Write the words in alphabetical (ABC) order.

book	cook	foot
good	look	put
stood	took	wood

_____   _____   _____
- - - - - - - - -   - - - - - - - - -   - - - - - - - - -
_____   _____   _____

_____   _____   _____
- - - - - - - - -   - - - - - - - - -   - - - - - - - - -
_____   _____   _____

(3) Write the sentences on the lines. Read each sentence.

_____

- -

I cook with wood.

_____

- -

The wood is good.

_____

- -

The cook is good.

_____

- -

I put my foot on their wood.

_____

- -

_____

- -

They put the wood on my foot.

_____

- -

_____

- -

I took a good look at their wood.

_____

- -

111

I stood on the wood with my foot.

Then I stood up.

I took a look.

They look at the cook with the book.

Then they took the book and the wood.

They took a good look at the cookbook.

(4) Write your own sentences using the spelling words.

(5) Listen to and write each spelling word.

_____   _____   _____
- - - - - - - - - -   - - - - - - - - - -   - - - - - - - - - -
_____   _____   _____

_____   _____   _____
- - - - - - - - - -   - - - - - - - - - -   - - - - - - - - - -
_____   _____   _____

_____   _____   _____
- - - - - - - - - -   - - - - - - - - - -   - - - - - - - - - -
_____   _____   _____

Review any words that you missed on the test.

_____   _____   _____
- - - - - - - - - -   - - - - - - - - - -   - - - - - - - - - -
_____   _____   _____

_____   _____   _____
- - - - - - - - - -   - - - - - - - - - -   - - - - - - - - - -
_____   _____   _____

_____   _____   _____
- - - - - - - - - -   - - - - - - - - - -   - - - - - - - - - -
_____   _____   _____

_____   _____   _____
- - - - - - - - - -   - - - - - - - - - -   - - - - - - - - - -
_____   _____   _____

_____   _____   _____
- - - - - - - - - -   - - - - - - - - - -   - - - - - - - - - -
_____   _____   _____

_____   _____   _____
- - - - - - - - - -   - - - - - - - - - -   - - - - - - - - - -
_____   _____   _____

List 19

<o> can spell [oʊ]. *Does* and *don't*. *Those* and *these*.

does	don't	goes
most	old	cold
hold	those	these

(1) Read each spelling word. Write each word three times.

does   The word *does* is the third person singular of the verb *do*. <Do + es -> does>
<o> spells [ʌ] like in the related *done*.

_____   _____   _____

- - - - - - - -   - - - - - - - -   - - - - - - - -

_____   _____   _____

don't   The word *don't* is a contraction of <do not>.

_____   _____   _____

- - - - - - - -   - - - - - - - -   - - - - - - - -

_____   _____   _____

goes   The word *goes* is the third person singular of the verb *go*. <Go + es -> does>

_____   _____   _____

- - - - - - - -   - - - - - - - -   - - - - - - - -

_____   _____   _____

most   <st> spells a consonant cluster.

_____   _____   _____

- - - - - - - -   - - - - - - - -   - - - - - - - -

_____   _____   _____

old   <ld> spells a consonant cluster.

_____   _____   _____

- - - - - - - -   - - - - - - - -   - - - - - - - -

_____   _____   _____

cold   <c> spells [k] before <a, o, u>.

_____   _____   _____

- - - - - - - -   - - - - - - - -   - - - - - - - -

_____   _____   _____

hold

those <th> is a digraph that spells [ð]. <s> spells [z]. The final <e> marks the <o> as spelling [oʊ].

these <th> is a digraph that spells [ð]. <s> spells [z]. The final <e> marks the first <e> as spelling [i].

(2) Write the words in alphabetical (ABC) order.

cold	does	don't
goes	hold	most
old	these	those

(3) Write the sentences on the lines. Read each sentence.

I am cold.

She is cold.

They are cold.

Most are cold.

He does it.

She does it.

I don't do it.

We don't do it.

They don't hold it.

Those are old.

These are old too.

I hold these.

You hold those.

Most are old.

Most were cold.

He goes there.

She goes there.

He goes to those.

She goes to these.

(4) Write your own sentences using the spelling words.

(5) Listen to and write each spelling word.

Review any words that you missed on the test.

<i> can spell [aɪ]. <a> can spell [eɪ].

did	big	six	give	gave
take	make	made	ate	came

(1) Read each spelling word. Write each word three times.

did   The word *did* is the simple past of the verb *do*. Relatives are *do*, *does*, and *done*.

big

six   <x> spells [ks].

give   The word *give* ends with a replaceable <e> to keep the word from ending with a <v>.

gave   The <e> marks the <a> as spelling [eɪ]. The word *gave* is the simple past of the verb *give*.

take   The word *take* is related to *took*.

make   The words *make* and *made* are related.

made The word *made* is the simple past and past participle of the verb *make*.

_____   _____   _____
- - - - - - - - - - - -   - - - - - - - - - - - -   - - - - - - - - - - - -
_____   _____   _____

ate The word *ate* is the simple past of the verb *eat*.

_____   _____   _____
- - - - - - - - - - - -   - - - - - - - - - - - -   - - - - - - - - - - - -
_____   _____   _____

came The word *came* is the simple past of the verb *come*.

_____   _____   _____
- - - - - - - - - - - -   - - - - - - - - - - - -   - - - - - - - - - - - -
_____   _____   _____

(2) Write the words in alphabetical (ABC) order.

ate	big	came	did	gave
give	made	make	six	take

_____   _____   _____
- - - - - - - - - - - -   - - - - - - - - - - - -   - - - - - - - - - - - -
_____   _____   _____

_____   _____   _____
- - - - - - - - - - - -   - - - - - - - - - - - -   - - - - - - - - - - - -
_____   _____   _____

_____   _____   _____
- - - - - - - - - - - -   - - - - - - - - - - - -   - - - - - - - - - - - -
_____   _____   _____

_____
- - - - - - - - - - - -
_____

(3) Write the sentences on the lines. Read each sentence.

_____

- -

_____

I am big.

_____

- -

_____

I did it.

_____

- -

_____

Give it to me.

_____

- -

_____

Give these to us.

_____

- -

_____

Give those to them.

_____

- -

_____

Take it to me.

_____

- -

_____

Take those to her.

_____

- -

_____

Take these to him.

_____

- -

_____

They made six.

They make six.

I ate six.

She ate six.

He ate six.

They came here.

We came too.

I gave six of those to you.

You gave six of these to me.

(4) Write your own sentences using the spelling words.

(5) Listen to and write each spelling word.

_____

- - - - - - - - - - - - -

_____

_____

- - - - - - - - - - - - -

_____

_____

- - - - - - - - - - - - -

_____

_____

- - - - - - - - - - - - -

_____

Review any words that you missed on the test.

126

List 21

<i> can spell [aɪ]. <ow> can spell [aʊ].

find	kind	mind
now	how	cow
wow	down	brown

(1) Read each spelling word. Write each word three times.

find   The word *find* is related to *found*. <nd> spells a consonant cluster.

_____   _____   _____

- - - - - - - - - - -   - - - - - - - - - - -   - - - - - - - - - - -

_____   _____   _____

kind

_____   _____   _____

- - - - - - - - - - -   - - - - - - - - - - -   - - - - - - - - - - -

_____   _____   _____

mind

_____   _____   _____

- - - - - - - - - - -   - - - - - - - - - - -   - - - - - - - - - - -

_____   _____   _____

now

_____   _____   _____

- - - - - - - - - - -   - - - - - - - - - - -   - - - - - - - - - - -

_____   _____   _____

how

_____   _____   _____

- - - - - - - - - - -   - - - - - - - - - - -   - - - - - - - - - - -

_____   _____   _____

cow   <c> spells [k] before <a, o, u>.

_____   _____   _____

- - - - - - - - - - -   - - - - - - - - - - -   - - - - - - - - - - -

_____   _____   _____

wow

down

brown
 spells a consonant cluster.

(2) Write the words in alphabetical (ABC) order.

brown	cow	down
find	how	kind
mind	now	wow

(3) Write the sentences on the lines. Read each sentence.

How are you?

How is she?

How old am I?

You are how old?

They are kind.

I find them kind.

I don't mind.

He does not mind.

I will find out.

We take it down.

I find a cow.

The cow is brown.

Wow! A brown cow!

The cow went down.

Mind the brown cow!

Find the brown cow!

Find the cow now!

How can you find a brown cow now?

(4) Write your own sentences using the spelling words.

(5) Listen to and write each spelling word.

Review any words that you missed on the test.

<a> can spell [æ].

man	ran	bad
than	ask	hand
fast	last	past

(1) Read each spelling word. Write each word three times.

man

_____ _____ _____
- - - - - - - - - - - - - - - - - - - - - - - - - - -
_____ _____ _____

ran

_____ _____ _____
- - - - - - - - - - - - - - - - - - - - - - - - - - -
_____ _____ _____

bad

_____ _____ _____
- - - - - - - - - - - - - - - - - - - - - - - - - - -
_____ _____ _____

than   <th> is a digraph that spells [ð].

_____ _____ _____
- - - - - - - - - - - - - - - - - - - - - - - - - - -
_____ _____ _____

ask   <sk> spells a consonant cluster.

_____ _____ _____
- - - - - - - - - - - - - - - - - - - - - - - - - - -
_____ _____ _____

hand   <nd> spells a consonant cluster.

_____ _____ _____
- - - - - - - - - - - - - - - - - - - - - - - - - - -
_____ _____ _____

fast <st> spells a consonant cluster.

_____
- - - - - - - - -
_____

last

_____
- - - - - - - - -
_____

past

_____
- - - - - - - - -
_____

(2) Write the words in alphabetical (ABC) order.

ask	bad	fast
hand	last	man
past	ran	than

(3) Write the sentences on the lines. Read each sentence.

_____

- -
_____

A man ran past.

_____

- -
_____

A man ran fast.

_____

- -
_____

A man ran last.

_____

- -
_____

They ran past.

_____

- -
_____

They ran fast.

_____

- -
_____

They ran last.

_____

- -
_____

The man was bad.

_____

- -
_____

Can I ask you?

_____

- -
_____

Can the man ask?

The man can ask me.

Ask the man.

Ask me last.

It was bad.

That was bad.

Some were bad.

Most are as big as a hand.

The man is as big as a cow.

(4) Write your own sentences using the spelling words.

(5) Listen to and write each spelling word.

_____ _____ _____
- - - - - - - - - - - - - - - - - - - - - - - - - - - - - - - - - - - - - -
_____ _____ _____

_____ _____ _____
- - - - - - - - - - - - - - - - - - - - - - - - - - - - - - - - - - - - - -
_____ _____ _____

_____ _____ _____
- - - - - - - - - - - - - - - - - - - - - - - - - - - - - - - - - - - - - -
_____ _____ _____

Review any words that you missed on the test.

_____ _____ _____
- - - - - - - - - - - - - - - - - - - - - - - - - - - - - - - - - - - - - -
_____ _____ _____

_____ _____ _____
- - - - - - - - - - - - - - - - - - - - - - - - - - - - - - - - - - - - - -
_____ _____ _____

_____ _____ _____
- - - - - - - - - - - - - - - - - - - - - - - - - - - - - - - - - - - - - -
_____ _____ _____

_____ _____ _____
- - - - - - - - - - - - - - - - - - - - - - - - - - - - - - - - - - - - - -
_____ _____ _____

_____ _____ _____
- - - - - - - - - - - - - - - - - - - - - - - - - - - - - - - - - - - - - -
_____ _____ _____

List 23

<e> can spell [ɛ].

ten	help	tell
sell	cell	fell
bell	yell	yellow

(1) Read each spelling word. Write each word three times.

ten

_____   _____   _____

- - - - - - - - - - -   - - - - - - - - - - -   - - - - - - - - - - -

_____   _____   _____

help   <lp> spells a consonant cluster.

_____   _____   _____

- - - - - - - - - - -   - - - - - - - - - - -   - - - - - - - - - - -

_____   _____   _____

tell   The <ll> marks a lexical spelling.

_____   _____   _____

- - - - - - - - - - -   - - - - - - - - - - -   - - - - - - - - - - -

_____   _____   _____

sell   The word *sell* means "to offer for sale."

_____   _____   _____

- - - - - - - - - - -   - - - - - - - - - - -   - - - - - - - - - - -

_____   _____   _____

cell   <c> spells [s] before <e, i, y>. The word *cell* means "a microscopic structure of a living being" and "a room in a prison or jail."

_____   _____   _____

- - - - - - - - - - -   - - - - - - - - - - -   - - - - - - - - - - -

_____   _____   _____

fell

_____   _____   _____

- - - - - - - - - - -   - - - - - - - - - - -   - - - - - - - - - - -

_____   _____   _____

bell

---

yell

---

yellow   <ow> is a digraph that spells [oʊ].

---

(2) Write the words in alphabetical (ABC) order.

bell	cell	fell
help	sell	tell
ten	yell	yellow

(3) Write the sentences on the lines. Read each sentence.

I sell ten.

I tell ten.

Ten are here.

A bell fell down.

The bell is yellow.

I see a cell.

The cell is yellow.

Ask them to help.

Tell them to help.

Ten yell too loud.

The ten are fast.

Ten ran past.

Ten fall down.

Ten help me out.

Some time will help.

Sell me the bell.

The bell is loud.

I tell ten to give a hand.

(4) Write your own sentences using the spelling words.

(5) Listen to and write each spelling word.

Review any words that you missed on the test.

List 24

<u> and <ew> can spell [u]. Replaceable <e> keeps a word from ending in <u>.

glue	due	blue
true	new	dew
blew	chew	grew

(1) Read each spelling word. Write each word three times.

glue <gl> spells a consonant cluster. The final <e> prevents the word from ending in <u>. Other suffixes can replace the <e>: *glued*, *gluing*, and *gluer*.

_____ _____ _____

- - - - - - - - - - - -   - - - - - - - - - - - -   - - - - - - - - - - - -

_____ _____ _____

due The words *due* and *dew* are homophones of *do*.
The word *due* means "owed or expected" and "an expected reward."

_____ _____ _____

- - - - - - - - - - - -   - - - - - - - - - - - -   - - - - - - - - - - - -

_____ _____ _____

blue The words *blue* and *blew* are homophones.
The word *blue* refers to the color.

_____ _____ _____

- - - - - - - - - - - -   - - - - - - - - - - - -   - - - - - - - - - - - -

_____ _____ _____

true The [tɹ] consonant cluster sounds similar to [t͡ʃɹ] because of the position of the tongue in the mouth for [t] and [ɹ].

_____ _____ _____

- - - - - - - - - - - -   - - - - - - - - - - - -   - - - - - - - - - - - -

_____ _____ _____

new The word *new* means "not old."

_____ _____ _____

- - - - - - - - - - - -   - - - - - - - - - - - -   - - - - - - - - - - - -

_____ _____ _____

dew   The word *dew* means "tiny drops of water that form on surfaces overnight."

_____   _____   _____

- - - - - - - - - -   - - - - - - - - - -   - - - - - - - - - -

_____   _____   _____

blew   The word *blew* is the simple past of the verb *blow*.

_____   _____   _____

- - - - - - - - - -   - - - - - - - - - -   - - - - - - - - - -

_____   _____   _____

chew   <ch> is a digraph that spells [t͡ʃ].

_____   _____   _____

- - - - - - - - - -   - - - - - - - - - -   - - - - - - - - - -

_____   _____   _____

grew   The word *grew* is the simple past of the verb *grow*.

_____   _____   _____

- - - - - - - - - -   - - - - - - - - - -   - - - - - - - - - -

_____   _____   _____

(2) Write the words in alphabetical (ABC) order.

blew	blue	chew
dew	due	glue
grew	new	true

_____   _____   _____

- - - - - - - - - -   - - - - - - - - - -   - - - - - - - - - -

_____   _____   _____

_____   _____   _____

- - - - - - - - - -   - - - - - - - - - -   - - - - - - - - - -

_____   _____   _____

(3) Write the sentences on the lines. Read each sentence.

I grew a blue one.

I chew a blue one.

I glue a new one.

The dew is new.

That is true.

That is not true.

The new one is blue.

She blew it.

He blew it.

It blew up.

The glue is new.

Chew it up!

Chew it good.

Glue it down.

The book is due.

It is still due.

The dew is wet.

The dew is cold.

The glue is wet.

(4) Write your own sentences using the spelling words.

(5) Listen to and write each spelling word.

_____   _____   _____
- - - - - - - - - -   - - - - - - - - - -   - - - - - - - - - -
_____   _____   _____

_____   _____   _____
- - - - - - - - - -   - - - - - - - - - -   - - - - - - - - - -
_____   _____   _____

_____   _____   _____
- - - - - - - - - -   - - - - - - - - - -   - - - - - - - - - -
_____   _____   _____

Review any words that you missed on the test.

_____   _____   _____
- - - - - - - - - -   - - - - - - - - - -   - - - - - - - - - -
_____   _____   _____

_____   _____   _____
- - - - - - - - - -   - - - - - - - - - -   - - - - - - - - - -
_____   _____   _____

_____   _____   _____
- - - - - - - - - -   - - - - - - - - - -   - - - - - - - - - -
_____   _____   _____

_____   _____   _____
- - - - - - - - - -   - - - - - - - - - -   - - - - - - - - - -
_____   _____   _____

_____   _____   _____
- - - - - - - - - -   - - - - - - - - - -   - - - - - - - - - -
_____   _____   _____

List 25

<u> can spell [ʌ].

run	fun	sun	cub	cut
nut	jump	just	must	much

(1) Read each spelling word. Write each word three times.

run   The word *run* is related to *ran*.

_____   _____   _____
- - - - - - - - -   - - - - - - - - -   - - - - - - - - -
_____   _____   _____

fun

_____   _____   _____
- - - - - - - - -   - - - - - - - - -   - - - - - - - - -
_____   _____   _____

sun   The word *sun* means "the star that the Earth orbits."

_____   _____   _____
- - - - - - - - -   - - - - - - - - -   - - - - - - - - -
_____   _____   _____

cub   <c> spells [k] before <a, o, u>.

_____   _____   _____
- - - - - - - - -   - - - - - - - - -   - - - - - - - - -
_____   _____   _____

cut   <c> spells [k] before <a, o, u>.

_____   _____   _____
- - - - - - - - -   - - - - - - - - -   - - - - - - - - -
_____   _____   _____

nut

_____   _____   _____
- - - - - - - - -   - - - - - - - - -   - - - - - - - - -
_____   _____   _____

jump   <mp> spells a consonant cluster.

_____   _____   _____
- - - - - - - - -   - - - - - - - - -   - - - - - - - - -
_____   _____   _____

151

just <st> spells a consonant cluster.

_____   _____   _____
- - - - - - - - -   - - - - - - - - -   - - - - - - - - -
_____   _____   _____

must <st> spells a consonant cluster.

_____   _____   _____
- - - - - - - - -   - - - - - - - - -   - - - - - - - - -
_____   _____   _____

much <ch> is a digraph that spells [tʃ].

_____   _____   _____
- - - - - - - - -   - - - - - - - - -   - - - - - - - - -
_____   _____   _____

(2) Write the words in alphabetical (ABC) order.

cub	cut	fun	jump	just
much	must	nut	run	sun

_____   _____   _____
- - - - - - - - -   - - - - - - - - -   - - - - - - - - -
_____   _____   _____

_____   _____   _____
- - - - - - - - -   - - - - - - - - -   - - - - - - - - -
_____   _____   _____

_____   _____   _____
- - - - - - - - -   - - - - - - - - -   - - - - - - - - -
_____   _____   _____

_____
- - - - - - - - -
_____

152

(3) Write the sentences on the lines. Read each sentence.

_____

- -

_____

I run fast.

_____

- -

_____

We run and jump.

_____

- -

_____

They just jump.

_____

- -

_____

He must jump.

_____

- -

_____

She must jump.

_____

- -

_____

Jump up in the sun!

_____

- -

_____

A cub can jump.

_____

- -

_____

A cub can run.

_____

- -

_____

The cub ate a nut.

They cut a nut.

I cut a nut too.

We just have fun.

They just had fun.

You must just jump.

The sun is fun.

The sun is much too hot.

They had too much fun in the sun.

(4) Write your own sentences using the spelling words.

(5) Listen to and write each spelling word.

Review any words that you missed on the test.

<ee> can spell [i]. *Been.*

keep	week	seem	feel	feet
need	green	sleep	queen	been

(1) Read each spelling word. Write each word three times.

keep

_____ _____ _____
- - - - - - - - - - - - - - - - - - - - - - - - - - -
_____ _____ _____

week The word *week* means "a time of seven days."

_____ _____ _____
- - - - - - - - - - - - - - - - - - - - - - - - - - -
_____ _____ _____

seem The word *seem* means "to appear" as in *You seem fine.*

_____ _____ _____
- - - - - - - - - - - - - - - - - - - - - - - - - - -
_____ _____ _____

feel

_____ _____ _____
- - - - - - - - - - - - - - - - - - - - - - - - - - -
_____ _____ _____

feet The word *feet* is the plural of the noun *foot.*

_____ _____ _____
- - - - - - - - - - - - - - - - - - - - - - - - - - -
_____ _____ _____

need The word *need* means "have to, must" and "something required."

_____ _____ _____
- - - - - - - - - - - - - - - - - - - - - - - - - - -
_____ _____ _____

green <gr> spells a consonant cluster.

_____ _____ _____
- - - - - - - - - - - - - - - - - - - - - - - - - - -
_____ _____ _____

sleep

<sl> spells a consonant cluster.

_____   _____   _____
- - - - - - - - - - - -   - - - - - - - - - - - -   - - - - - - - - - - - -
_____   _____   _____

queen

<qu> is a digraph that spells [kw].

_____   _____   _____
- - - - - - - - - - - -   - - - - - - - - - - - -   - - - - - - - - - - - -
_____   _____   _____

been

The word *been* is the past participle of the verb *be*. <Be + en -> been> The vowel is [i] or [ɛ].

_____   _____   _____
- - - - - - - - - - - -   - - - - - - - - - - - -   - - - - - - - - - - - -
_____   _____   _____

(2) Write the words in alphabetical (ABC) order.

been	feel	feet	green	keep
need	queen	seem	sleep	week

_____   _____   _____
- - - - - - - - - - - -   - - - - - - - - - - - -   - - - - - - - - - - - -
_____   _____   _____

_____   _____   _____
- - - - - - - - - - - -   - - - - - - - - - - - -   - - - - - - - - - - - -
_____   _____   _____

_____
- - - - - - - - - - - -
_____

(3) Write the sentences on the lines. Read each sentence.

_____

- -
_____

I need sleep.

_____

- -
_____

We need sleep.

_____

- -
_____

They need sleep.

_____

- -
_____

I feel ill.

_____

- -
_____

You feel ill.

_____

- -
_____

We seem sad.

_____

- -
_____

They seem sad.

_____

- -
_____

Keep up with me.

_____

- -
_____

Keep just some.

159

My feet need sleep.

My feet are hot.

My feet are cold.

It is green.

They are green.

A queen has been here.

A queen has been there.

Where has the queen been?

The week is here.

The week was good.

(4) Write your own sentences using the spelling words.

(5) Listen to and write each spelling word.

Review any words that you missed on the test.

List 27

<a> can spell [ɔ]. Compound words *also*, *into*, *onto*, and *upon*.

wash	want	water
warm	warn	also
into	onto	upon

(1) Read each spelling word. Write each word three times.

wash   <sh> is a digraph that spells [ʃ].

_____   _____   _____

- - - - - - - - -   - - - - - - - - -   - - - - - - - - -

_____   _____   _____

want   <nt> spells a consonant cluster.

_____   _____   _____

- - - - - - - - -   - - - - - - - - -   - - - - - - - - -

_____   _____   _____

water

_____   _____   _____

- - - - - - - - -   - - - - - - - - -   - - - - - - - - -

_____   _____   _____

warm   <rm> spells a consonant cluster.

_____   _____   _____

- - - - - - - - -   - - - - - - - - -   - - - - - - - - -

_____   _____   _____

warn   <rn> spells a consonant cluster.

_____   _____   _____

- - - - - - - - -   - - - - - - - - -   - - - - - - - - -

_____   _____   _____

also   <al + So -> also> Compare *already*, *always*, and *alone*.

_____   _____   _____

- - - - - - - - -   - - - - - - - - -   - - - - - - - - -

_____   _____   _____

into   <In + To -> into>

onto   <On + To -> onto>

upon   <Up + On -> upon>

(2) Write the words in alphabetical (ABC) order.

also	into	onto
upon	want	warm
warn	wash	water

(3) Write the sentences on the lines. Read each sentence.

_____

- -

_____

I wash with some warm water.

_____

- -

_____

We want to wash.

_____

- -

They want to wash.

_____

- -

I will warn you.

_____

- -

You must warn me.

_____

- -

Jump into the water.

_____

- -

Also jump out.

_____

- -

Jump onto the green.

Sleep upon the bed.

Go into the water.

Jump onto the cow.

The water was warm.

The queen is warm.

You are also warm.

Once upon a time, the queen sat upon the dew in the sun.

(4) Write your own sentences using the spelling words.

(5) Listen to and write each spelling word.

Review any words that you missed on the test.

List 28

<aw> can spell [ɑ]. <ow> can spell [oʊ]. <ew> can spell [u] an [ju].

saw	raw	paw	draw	grow
show	know	knew	drew	few

(1) Read each spelling word. Write each word three times.

saw   The word *saw* is the simple past of the verb *see*.

_____   _____   _____
- - - - - - - - - -   - - - - - - - - - -   - - - - - - - - - -
_____   _____   _____

raw

_____   _____   _____
- - - - - - - - - -   - - - - - - - - - -   - - - - - - - - - -
_____   _____   _____

paw

_____   _____   _____
- - - - - - - - - -   - - - - - - - - - -   - - - - - - - - - -
_____   _____   _____

drew   The <dr> consonant cluster sounds like [d͡ʒɹ] because of the position of the tongue in the mouth for [d] and [ɹ].

_____   _____   _____
- - - - - - - - - -   - - - - - - - - - -   - - - - - - - - - -
_____   _____   _____

grow   The word *grow* is related to the verb *grew*. <gr> spells a consonant cluster.

_____   _____   _____
- - - - - - - - - -   - - - - - - - - - -   - - - - - - - - - -
_____   _____   _____

show   <sh> is a digraph that spells [ʃ].

_____   _____   _____
- - - - - - - - - -   - - - - - - - - - -   - - - - - - - - - -

know <kn> is a digraph that spells [n]. The word *know* is a homophone of *no*.

---

knew The word *knew* is the simple past of the verb *know*. The word *knew* is a homophone of *new*.

---

drew The word *drew* is the simple past of the verb *drew*.

---

few The <ew> in *few* spells [ju].

---

(2) Write the words in alphabetical (ABC) order.

draw	drew	few	grew	grow
knew	know	paw	raw	show

(3) Write the sentences on the lines. Read each sentence.

They saw a show.

I grow a few.

I grew a few.

They seem raw.

Those are raw.

These are raw.

Mine is raw also..

I know a few.

I knew a few.

A few grow.

A few grew.

Show me a paw.

They show me a paw.

I draw the paw.

I drew the paw.

I saw its paw.

Its paw is raw.

Put warm water onto its raw paw.

(4) Write your own sentences using the spelling words.

(5) Listen to and write each spelling word.

_____

_____

_____

_____

Review any words that you missed on the test.

_____

_____

_____

_____

List 29

Any and *many*. <our> can spell [ɔɹ]. <ea> can spell [i].

any	many	four	pour	your
eat	ear	year	clean	read

(1) Read each spelling word. Write each word three times.

any   The <a> in *any* can spell [æ] or be reduced to [ɛ] or [ə].

_____   _____   _____
- - - - - - - - - -   - - - - - - - - - -   - - - - - - - - - -
_____   _____   _____

many   The <a> in *many* can spell [æ] or be reduced to [ɛ] or [ə]. The pronunciation was influenced by *any*.

_____   _____   _____
- - - - - - - - - -   - - - - - - - - - -   - - - - - - - - - -
_____   _____   _____

four   The word *four* means the number. *Four* is a homophone of *for*.

_____   _____   _____
- - - - - - - - - -   - - - - - - - - - -   - - - - - - - - - -
_____   _____   _____

pour   The word *pour* is a homophone or *pore* and *poor*.

_____   _____   _____
- - - - - - - - - -   - - - - - - - - - -   - - - - - - - - - -
_____   _____   _____

your

_____   _____   _____
- - - - - - - - - -   - - - - - - - - - -   - - - - - - - - - -
_____   _____   _____

eat   The word *eat* is related to the word *ate*.

_____   _____   _____
- - - - - - - - - -   - - - - - - - - - -   - - - - - - - - - -
_____   _____   _____

ear

_____   _____   _____
- - - - - - - - - -   - - - - - - - - - -   - - - - - - - - - -
_____   _____   _____

year

_____   _____   _____
- - - - - - - - - -   - - - - - - - - - -   - - - - - - - - - -
_____   _____   _____

clean <cl> spells a consonant cluster.

_____   _____   _____
- - - - - - - - - -   - - - - - - - - - -   - - - - - - - - - -
_____   _____   _____

read   The <ea> in *read* spells both [i] and [ɛ].

_____   _____   _____
- - - - - - - - - -   - - - - - - - - - -   - - - - - - - - - -
_____   _____   _____

(2) Write the words in alphabetical (ABC) order.

any	clean	ear	eat	four
many	pour	read	year	your

_____   _____   _____
- - - - - - - - - -   - - - - - - - - - -   - - - - - - - - - -
_____   _____   _____

_____   _____   _____
- - - - - - - - - -   - - - - - - - - - -   - - - - - - - - - -
_____   _____   _____

_____   _____   _____
- - - - - - - - - -   - - - - - - - - - -   - - - - - - - - - -
_____   _____   _____

_____
- - - - - - - - - -
_____

(3) Write the sentences on the lines. Read each sentence.

_____

- -

_____

Pour your water.

_____

- -

_____

Read a good book.

_____

- -

_____

Eat some now.

_____

- -

_____

Eat four now.

_____

- -

_____

The year is here.

_____

- -

_____

Four can eat.

_____

- -

_____

Many can eat.

_____

- -

_____

You can eat many.

_____

- -

_____

You can eat any.

Clean your ear.

Pour some water.

Clean and then eat.

Clean what you eat.

Read any and many.

I also read.

Read all year.

Also read all day.

Read all the time.

You can read your four.

(4) Write your own sentences using the spelling words.

(5) Listen to and write each spelling word.

Review any words that you missed on the test.

List 30

<ck> spells [k] at the end of a morpheme.

black	back	sack	sock	rock
duck	pick	sick	kick	neck

(1) Read each spelling word. Write each word three times.

black <bl> spells a consonant cluster.

_____   _____   _____

- - - - - - - - - - - -   - - - - - - - - - - - -   - - - - - - - - - - - -

_____   _____   _____

back

_____   _____   _____

- - - - - - - - - - - -   - - - - - - - - - - - -   - - - - - - - - - - - -

_____   _____   _____

sack

_____   _____   _____

- - - - - - - - - - - -   - - - - - - - - - - - -   - - - - - - - - - - - -

_____   _____   _____

sock

_____   _____   _____

- - - - - - - - - - - -   - - - - - - - - - - - -   - - - - - - - - - - - -

_____   _____   _____

rock

_____   _____   _____

- - - - - - - - - - - -   - - - - - - - - - - - -   - - - - - - - - - - - -

_____   _____   _____

duck

_____   _____   _____

- - - - - - - - - - - -   - - - - - - - - - - - -   - - - - - - - - - - - -

_____   _____   _____

pick

_____   _____   _____

- - - - - - - - - - - -   - - - - - - - - - - - -   - - - - - - - - - - - -

_____   _____   _____

sick

pick

neck

(2) Write the words in alphabetical (ABC) order.

back	black	duck	kick	neck
pick	rock	sack	sick	sock

(3) Write the sentences on the lines. Read each sentence.

_____

- -

Pick a rock.

_____

- -

Pick a sack.

_____

- -

Pick a sock.

_____

- -

My sock is black.

_____

- -

I am sick.

_____

- -

You are sick.

_____

- -

They are sick.

_____

- -

The rock is black.

_____

- -

The duck is black.

Clean the duck.

Pet the duck.

Do not kick the clean black duck.

Look at your neck.

See my neck too.

Put the rock in the sock.

Put the rock in the sack.

Give my rock back.

Put the rock back.

(4) Write your own sentences using the spelling words.

(5) Listen to and write each spelling word.

Review any words that you missed on the test.

<o> can spell [ɔ].

dog	frog	box	fox	mom
job	hop	pop	top	stop

(1) Read each spelling word. Write each word three times.

dog

_____ _____ _____
- -
_____ _____ _____

frog   <fr> spells a consonant cluster.

_____ _____ _____
- -
_____ _____ _____

box   <x> spells [ks]

_____ _____ _____
- -
_____ _____ _____

fox

_____ _____ _____
- -
_____ _____ _____

mom

_____ _____ _____
- -
_____ _____ _____

job

_____ _____ _____
- -
_____ _____ _____

hop

_____ _____ _____
- -
_____ _____ _____

pop

_____   _____   _____
- - - - - - - - -   - - - - - - - - - - - - - - - - - -
_____   _____   _____

top

_____   _____   _____
- - - - - - - - -   - - - - - - - - - - - - - - - - - -
_____   _____   _____

stop   <st> spells a consonant cluster.

_____   _____   _____
- - - - - - - - -   - - - - - - - - - - - - - - - - - -
_____   _____   _____

(2) Write the words in alphabetical (ABC) order.

box	dog	fox	frog	hop
job	mom	pop	stop	top

_____   _____   _____
- - - - - - - - -   - - - - - - - - - - - - - - - - - -
_____   _____   _____

_____   _____   _____
- - - - - - - - -   - - - - - - - - - - - - - - - - - -
_____   _____   _____

_____   _____   _____
- - - - - - - - -   - - - - - - - - - - - - - - - - - -
_____   _____   _____

_____
- - - - - - - - -
_____

(3) Write the sentences on the lines. Read each sentence.

_____

- -

A dog and frog are in a box.

_____

- -

_____

- -

A fox will stop and hop.

_____

- -

_____

- -

Mom got a new job.

_____

- -

The box is on top.

_____

- -

Hop on top.

_____

- -

The job must stop.

_____

- -

The fox is black.

Mom can hop.

Mom can stop.

Pop can hop.

Pop can stop.

The fox will hop into the box.

The frog will hop upon the box top.

The dog will stop the fox and frog.

(4) Write your own sentences using the spelling words.

(5) Listen to and write each spelling word.

Review any words that you missed on the test.

<oa> can spell [oʊ].

oat	boat	coat	float	oak
loaf	toad	road	soap	soak

(1) Read each spelling word. Write each word three times.

oat

_____   _____   _____

- - - - - - - - - - - - - - -   - - - - - - - - - - - - - - -   - - - - - - - - - - - - - - -

_____   _____   _____

boat

_____   _____   _____

- - - - - - - - - - - - - - -   - - - - - - - - - - - - - - -   - - - - - - - - - - - - - - -

_____   _____   _____

coat

_____   _____   _____

- - - - - - - - - - - - - - -   - - - - - - - - - - - - - - -   - - - - - - - - - - - - - - -

_____   _____   _____

float <fl> spells a consonant cluster.

_____   _____   _____

- - - - - - - - - - - - - - -   - - - - - - - - - - - - - - -   - - - - - - - - - - - - - - -

_____   _____   _____

oak

_____   _____   _____

- - - - - - - - - - - - - - -   - - - - - - - - - - - - - - -   - - - - - - - - - - - - - - -

_____   _____   _____

loaf

_____   _____   _____

- - - - - - - - - - - - - - -   - - - - - - - - - - - - - - -   - - - - - - - - - - - - - - -

_____   _____   _____

toad

_____   _____   _____

- - - - - - - - - - - - - - -   - - - - - - - - - - - - - - -   - - - - - - - - - - - - - - -

_____   _____   _____

road

soap

soak

(2) Write the words in alphabetical (ABC) order.

boat	coat	float	loaf	oak
oat	road	soak	soap	toad

(3) Write the sentences on the lines. Read each sentence.

_____

- -

A toad ate an oat.

_____

- -

A toad ate a loaf.

_____

- -

My boat can float.

_____

- -

Your boat can float.

_____

- -

Have a good soak.

_____

- -

Soak with some soap.

_____

- -

Put on a coat.

_____

- -

A toad is in the road.

_____

- -

An oak is by the road.

A toad is by the oak.

Eat an oat loaf.

I ate an oat loaf.

Stop by the road.

Stop at the oak.

Float in a boat.

Let the soap float.

Soak the soap well.

The oak is old.

The road is old.

(4) Write your own sentences using the spelling words.

(5) Listen to and write each spelling word.

Review any words that you missed on the test.

List 33

<oo> can spell [u]. <u> can spell [ju].

zoo	soon	moon	noon	spoon
boot	room	mood	use	fuse

(1) Read each spelling word. Write each word three times.

zoo

_____   _____   _____

- - - - - - - - - -   - - - - - - - - - -   - - - - - - - - - -

_____   _____   _____

soon

_____   _____   _____

- - - - - - - - - -   - - - - - - - - - -   - - - - - - - - - -

_____   _____   _____

moon

_____   _____   _____

- - - - - - - - - -   - - - - - - - - - -   - - - - - - - - - -

_____   _____   _____

noon

_____   _____   _____

- - - - - - - - - -   - - - - - - - - - -   - - - - - - - - - -

_____   _____   _____

spoon   <sp> spells a consonant cluster.

_____   _____   _____

- - - - - - - - - -   - - - - - - - - - -   - - - - - - - - - -

_____   _____   _____

boot

_____   _____   _____

- - - - - - - - - -   - - - - - - - - - -   - - - - - - - - - -

_____   _____   _____

room

_____   _____   _____

- - - - - - - - - -   - - - - - - - - - -   - - - - - - - - - -

_____   _____   _____

mood

_____   _____   _____
- - - - - - - - -   - - - - - - - - -   - - - - - - - - -
_____   _____   _____

use   The replaceable <e> marks the sound of the <u>.

_____   _____   _____
- - - - - - - - -   - - - - - - - - -   - - - - - - - - -
_____   _____   _____

fuse   The replaceable <e> marks the sound of the <u>.

_____   _____   _____
- - - - - - - - -   - - - - - - - - -   - - - - - - - - -
_____   _____   _____

(2) Write the words in alphabetical (ABC) order.

boot	fuse	mood	moon	noon
room	spoon	soon	use	zoo

_____   _____   _____
- - - - - - - - -   - - - - - - - - -   - - - - - - - - -
_____   _____   _____

_____   _____   _____
- - - - - - - - -   - - - - - - - - -   - - - - - - - - -
_____   _____   _____

_____   _____   _____
- - - - - - - - -   - - - - - - - - -   - - - - - - - - -
_____   _____   _____

_____
- - - - - - - - -
_____

(3) Write the sentences on the lines. Read each sentence.

They go to the zoo at noon.

The man goes to the zoo at noon.

I need a spoon.

We need some room.

I use a spoon.

I found my boot in my room.

The moon is out.

The moon will come soon.

He is in a mood.

She is in a mood.

We can fuse it.

They can fuse it.

Noon is soon.

Mom will stop soon.

Mom will stop at noon.

It will come soon.

(4) Write your own sentences using the spelling words.

(5) Listen to and write each spelling word.

_____ _____ _____

_____ _____ _____

_____ _____ _____

_____

Review any words that you missed on the test.

_____ _____ _____

_____ _____ _____

_____ _____ _____

_____ _____ _____

<y> and <ye> can spell [aɪ].

fly	fry	sky
sly	spy	guy
buy	bye	eye

(1) Read each spelling word. Write each word three times.

fly   <fl> spells a consonant cluster.

_____   _____   _____

- - - - - - - - - -   - - - - - - - - - -   - - - - - - - - - -

_____   _____   _____

fry   <fr> spells a consonant cluster.

_____   _____   _____

- - - - - - - - - -   - - - - - - - - - -   - - - - - - - - - -

_____   _____   _____

sky   <sk> spells a consonant cluster.

_____   _____   _____

- - - - - - - - - -   - - - - - - - - - -   - - - - - - - - - -

_____   _____   _____

sly   <sl> spells a consonant cluster.

_____   _____   _____

- - - - - - - - - -   - - - - - - - - - -   - - - - - - - - - -

_____   _____   _____

spy   <sp> spells a consonant cluster.

_____   _____   _____

- - - - - - - - - -   - - - - - - - - - -   - - - - - - - - - -

_____   _____   _____

guy   <gu> is a digraph that spells [g]. Compare *guide* and *guess*.

_____   _____   _____

- - - - - - - - - -   - - - - - - - - - -   - - - - - - - - - -

_____   _____   _____

buy   The <u> is an etymological marker that marks a relationship with the <ugh> in *bought*.

_____   _____   _____
- - - - - - - - -   - - - - - - - - -   - - - - - - - - -
_____   _____   _____

bye   <ye> is a digraph that spells [aɪ]. *Bye, buy,* and *by* are homophones.

_____   _____   _____
- - - - - - - - -   - - - - - - - - -   - - - - - - - - -
_____   _____   _____

eye   <ye> is a digraph that spells [aɪ]. The first <e> is a lexical marker. *Eye* is a homophone if *I*.

_____   _____   _____
- - - - - - - - -   - - - - - - - - -   - - - - - - - - -
_____   _____   _____

(2) Write the words in alphabetical (ABC) order.

buy	bye	eye
fly	fry	guy
sky	sly	spy

_____   _____   _____
- - - - - - - - -   - - - - - - - - -   - - - - - - - - -
_____   _____   _____

_____   _____   _____
- - - - - - - - -   - - - - - - - - -   - - - - - - - - -
_____   _____   _____

_____   _____   _____
- - - - - - - - -   - - - - - - - - -   - - - - - - - - -
_____   _____   _____

(3) Write the sentences on the lines. Read each sentence.

_____

- -

_____

I will fly at noon.

_____

- -

_____

It may fly soon.

_____

- -

_____

The guy will fly.

_____

- -

_____

You can fry it.

_____

- -

_____

We must fry it.

_____

- -

_____

The sky is blue.

_____

- -

_____

The sky is gray.

_____

- -

_____

The fox is sly.

_____

- -

_____

I buy a sly fox.

That guy is sly.

The guy is a spy.

I spy a sly spy with my eye.

I say bye.

She says bye.

He says bye too.

I use my eye.

I spy a blue sky with my eye.

(4) Write your own sentences using the spelling words.

(5) Listen to and write each spelling word.

Review any words that you missed on the test.

List 35

<a> can spell [æ].

cat	sat	mat	hat	bat
mad	dad	pan	nap	map

(1) Read each spelling word. Write each word three times.

cat

_____   _____   _____

- - - - - - - - - - - - - - - - -   - - - - - - - - - - - - - - - - -   - - - - - - - - - - - - - - - - -

_____   _____   _____

sat

_____   _____   _____

- - - - - - - - - - - - - - - - -   - - - - - - - - - - - - - - - - -   - - - - - - - - - - - - - - - - -

_____   _____   _____

mat

_____   _____   _____

- - - - - - - - - - - - - - - - -   - - - - - - - - - - - - - - - - -   - - - - - - - - - - - - - - - - -

_____   _____   _____

hat

_____   _____   _____

- - - - - - - - - - - - - - - - -   - - - - - - - - - - - - - - - - -   - - - - - - - - - - - - - - - - -

_____   _____   _____

bat

_____   _____   _____

- - - - - - - - - - - - - - - - -   - - - - - - - - - - - - - - - - -   - - - - - - - - - - - - - - - - -

_____   _____   _____

mad

_____   _____   _____

- - - - - - - - - - - - - - - - -   - - - - - - - - - - - - - - - - -   - - - - - - - - - - - - - - - - -

_____   _____   _____

dad

_____   _____   _____

- - - - - - - - - - - - - - - - -   - - - - - - - - - - - - - - - - -   - - - - - - - - - - - - - - - - -

_____   _____   _____

pan

_____   _____   _____
- - - - - - - - -   - - - - - - - - -   - - - - - - - - -
_____   _____   _____

nap

_____   _____   _____
- - - - - - - - -   - - - - - - - - -   - - - - - - - - -
_____   _____   _____

map

_____   _____   _____
- - - - - - - - -   - - - - - - - - -   - - - - - - - - -
_____   _____   _____

(2) Write the words in alphabetical (ABC) order.

bat	cat	dad	hat	mad
map	mat	nap	pan	sat

_____   _____   _____
- - - - - - - - -   - - - - - - - - -   - - - - - - - - -
_____   _____   _____

_____   _____   _____
- - - - - - - - -   - - - - - - - - -   - - - - - - - - -
_____   _____   _____

_____   _____   _____
- - - - - - - - -   - - - - - - - - -   - - - - - - - - -
_____   _____   _____

_____
- - - - - - - - -
_____

(3) Write the sentences on the lines. Read each sentence.

A cat sat on a map on a mat.

A bat took a nap on a mat.

Dad has a pan.

Dad took a nap.

Dad can use a map.

Dad will use a pan.

Dad has a hat.

The cat sat on top of dad.

Dad sat on top of the cat.

The cat got mad.

Now the cat is so mad at dad.

Does dad feel bad?

He does feel bad.

Dad puts on his hat.

He lets the cat nap.

Dad lets the cat take a nap on him.

(4) Write your own sentences using the spelling words.

(5) Listen to and write each spelling word.

Review any words that you missed on the test.

List 36

<n> can spell [ŋ]. <g> can spell [Ø]. <g> and <k> can mark <n> as spelling [ŋ].

long	song	wrong	sing	bring
thing	pink	think	drink	thank

(1) Read each spelling word. Write each word three times.

long   The <g> is zeroed and marks the <n> as spelling [ŋ].

song

wrong   <wr> is a digraph that spells [ɹ].

sing

bring
 spells a consonant cluster.

thing   <th> is a digraph that spells [θ].

pink   The <k> spells [k] and marks the <n> as spelling [ŋ].

think

<th> is a digraph that spells [θ].

_____   _____   _____
- - - - - - - - - -   - - - - - - - - - -   - - - - - - - - - -
_____   _____   _____

drink

The <dr> consonant cluster sounds like [d͡ʒɹ] because of the position of the tongue in the mouth for [d] and [ɹ].

_____   _____   _____
- - - - - - - - - -   - - - - - - - - - -   - - - - - - - - - -
_____   _____   _____

thank

<th> is a digraph that spells [θ].

_____   _____   _____
- - - - - - - - - -   - - - - - - - - - -   - - - - - - - - - -
_____   _____   _____

(2) Write the words in alphabetical (ABC) order.

bring	drink	long	pink	sing
song	thank	thing	think	wrong

_____   _____   _____
- - - - - - - - - -   - - - - - - - - - -   - - - - - - - - - -
_____   _____   _____

_____   _____   _____
- - - - - - - - - -   - - - - - - - - - -   - - - - - - - - - -
_____   _____   _____

_____   _____   _____
- - - - - - - - - -   - - - - - - - - - -   - - - - - - - - - -
_____   _____   _____

_____
- - - - - - - - - -
_____

218

(3) Write the sentences on the lines. Read each sentence.

I sing a song.

Sing a long song.

I bring a drink.

The drink is pink.

I must think.

I am not wrong.

I think about how I sing a long song.

I must thank you.

219

Bring me that thing.

I think that is the wrong thing.

Bring me the pink thing.

Bring me a drink too.

Thank you for the pink drink!

I think the pink drink is just the thing!

Thank you so much!

(4) Write your own sentences using the spelling words.

(5) Listen to and write each spelling word.

Review any words that you missed on the test.

Master List

List 1

Function words. <e> can spell [i].
A digraph is two letters that spell
one sound.

1. a
2. an
3. I
4. the
5. be
6. me
7. he
8. she
9. we

List 2

<i> can spell [ɪ].

1. it
2. its
3. it's
4. in
5. if
6. is
7. him
8. his

List 3

<a> can spell [æ].

1. am
2. at
3. as
4. and
5. that
6. have
7. has
8. had
9. can

List 4

<u> and <a> can spell [ʌ]. <o>
can spell [ʌ] before <m>, <n>,
<u>, and <v>.

1. us
2. up
3. but
4. was
5. what
6. come
7. some
8. done
9. none

List 5

<o> can spell [oʊ] and [ɑ].

1. no
2. so
3. go
4. gone
5. on
6. not
7. pot
8. lot
9. got
10. hot

List 6

<ar> can spell [ɑɹ]. <er> can
spell [ɜɹ].

1. are
2. car
3. bar
4. jar
5. far
6. were
7. her
8. hers

List 7

<o>, <oo>, and <ou> can spell
[u].

1. do
2. to
3. too
4. two
5. who
6. you
7. your
8. yours

List 8

<o> can spell [ʷʌ]. <y> can spell
[ɑɪ].

1. one
2. once
3. by
4. my
5. why
6. shy
7. cry
8. try
9. dry

List 9

<o> can spell [ʌ] before <m>,
<n>, <u>, and <v>. <o> can spell
[ɔ].

1. of
2. off
3. from
4. come
5. some
6. love
7. or
8. for
9. nor

List 10

<i> can spell [ɪ].

1. with
2. this
3. bit
4. fit
5. sit
6. hit
7. pit
8. lit
9. kit

List 11

<i> can spell [ɪ]. <a> can spell [ɔ]. <ll> spells [l]. <l> can mark <a> as spelling [ɔ].

1. will
2. ill
3. still
4. all
5. ball
6. call
7. fall
8. hall
9. tall

List 12

They, them, their, and *theirs.* <e> can spell [ɛ].

1. they
2. them
3. their
4. theirs
5. get
6. let
7. jet
8. pet
9. wet
10. met

List 13

<ay> can spell [eɪ].

1. say
2. may
3. way
4. day
5. pay
6. bay
7. stay
8. play
9. gray

List 14

Here, there, and *where.* <ee> can spell [i].

1. here
2. there
3. where
4. see
5. bee
6. free
7. tree
8. three

List 15

Replaceable <e> can mark <i> as spelling [ɑɪ].

1. ride
2. life
3. bike
4. like
5. time
6. line
7. mine
8. fine
9. nine
10. five

List 16

<ou> can spell [ɑʊ].

1. out
2. about
3. loud
4. cloud
5. found
6. sound
7. our
8. ours
9. hour

List 17

Says and *said.* <e> can spell [ɛ].

1. says
2. said
3. when
4. then
5. well
6. red
7. bed
8. set
9. yes
10. went

List 18

<oo> and <u> can spell [ʊ].

1. book
2. cook
3. look
4. took
5. foot
6. good
7. wood
8. stood
9. put

List 19

<o> can spell [oʊ]. *Does* and *don't*. *Those* and *these*.

1. does
2. don't
3. goes
4. most
5. old
6. cold
7. hold
8. those
9. these

List 20

<i> can spell [aɪ]. <a> can spell [eɪ].

1. did
2. big
3. six
4. give
5. gave
6. take
7. make
8. made
9. ate
10. came

List 21

<i> can spell [aɪ]. <ow> can spell [aʊ].

1. find
2. kind
3. mind
4. now
5. how
6. cow
7. wow
8. down
9. brown

List 22

<a> can spell [æ].

1. man
2. ran
3. bad
4. than
5. ask
6. hand
7. fast
8. last
9. past

List 23

<e> can spell [ɛ].

1. ten
2. help
3. tell
4. sell
5. cell
6. fell
7. bell
8. yell
9. yellow

List 24

<u> and <ew> can spell [u]. Replaceable <e> keeps a word from ending in <u>.

1. glue
2. due
3. blue
4. true
5. new
6. dew
7. blew
8. chew
9. grew

List 25

<u> can spell [ʌ].

1. run
2. fun
3. sun
4. cub
5. cut
6. nut
7. jump
8. must
9. just
10. much

List 26

<ee> can spell [i]. *Been*.

1. keep
2. week
3. seem
4. feel
5. feet
6. need
7. green
8. sleep
9. queen
10. been

List 27

<a> can spell [ɔ]. Compound words *also*, *into*, *onto*, and *upon*.

1. wash
2. want
3. water
4. warm
5. warn
6. also
7. into
8. onto
9. upon

List 28

<aw> can spell [ɑ]. <ow> can spell [oʊ]. <ew> can spell [u] an [ju].

1. saw
2. raw
3. paw
4. draw
5. show
6. grow
7. grew
8. know
9. knew
10. few

List 29

Any and *many*. <our> can spell [ɔɹ]. <ea> can spell [i].

1. any
2. many
3. four
4. pour
5. your
6. eat
7. ear
8. year
9. clean
10. read*

List 30

<ck> spells [k] at the end of a morpheme.

1. back
2. black
3. sack
4. sock
5. rock
6. duck
7. pick
8. sick
9. kick
10. neck

List 31

<o> can spell [ɔ].

1. dog
2. frog
3. box
4. fox
5. mom
6. job
7. hop
8. pop
9. top
10. stop

List 32

<oa> can spell [oʊ].

1. oat
2. boat
3. coat
4. float
5. oak
6. loaf
7. toad
8. road
9. soap
10. soak

List 33

<oo> can spell [u]. <u> can spell [ju].

1. zoo
2. soon
3. moon
4. noon
5. spoon
6. boot
7. room
8. mood
9. use
10. fuse

List 34

<y> and <ye> can spell [ɑɪ].

1. fly
2. fry
3. sky
4. sly
5. spy
6. guy
7. buy
8. bye
9. eye

List 35

<a> can spell [æ].

1. cat
2. sat
3. mat
4. hat
5. bat
6. mad
7. dad
8. pan
9. nap
10. map

List 36

<n> can spell [ŋ]. <g> can spell [Ø]. <g> and <k> can mark <n> as spelling [ŋ].

1. long
2. song
3. wrong
4. sing
5. bring
6. thing
7. pink
8. think
9. drink
10. thank

About the Author

Heather Marie Kosur earned a BA in English studies with a minor in creative writing in May 2007 from Illinois State University, an MS in library and information science in May 2009 from the University of Illinois at Urbana-Champaign, and an MS in English studies with an emphasis in linguistics in December 2011 from Illinois State University. She wrote her English studies thesis on multiple modals in American English entitled *Structure and Meaning of Periphrastic Modal Verbs in Modern American English: Multiple Modals as Single-Unit Constructions*. She is also the author of the *Teach a Student to Read* reading program and *A Form-Function Description of the Grammar of the Modern English Language for Junior High*. Her academic passions include English grammar and English spelling.

About TASTR

Teach a Student to Read (TASTR) developed in response to the Teach Your Child to Read in 100 Easy Lessons reading program. Unlike phonics programs that erroneously posit that sounds correlate with letters in an alphabetic writing system, TASTR strives to teach the English writing system as fully and accurately as possible.

TASTR approaches the teaching of reading through the tenet that the primary function of English spelling is to express meaning. The program begins with the expectation that the reading student knows the letters of the English alphabet and then teaches the graphemes of the English spelling system. The student learns about the graphemes, digraphs, and trigraphs that can spell sounds. But not all letters spell sounds. Some letters are markers. Other letters are zeroed. The single final nonsyllabic E, which is the lynchpin of the English spelling system, is introduced in the first lesson. A student must understand that not all letters spell sounds as soon as learning to read begins.

In addition to English graphemes, TASTR also introduces word sums, prefixes, and suffixes. A word sum shows how a word is built. The student will learn the ways that prefixes and suffixes affect the spelling and pronunciation of words.

TASTR additionally includes information about some of the most common verbs in English as well as information about nouns, adjectives, and adverbs. A brief tutorial for uncovering the history of a word, and thus an explanation of the spelling, is included in the introduction.

Teach a Student to Read is not a phonics program. TASTR presents English orthography as fully and accurately as possible, thus giving a new reader the information needed to read and understand the spelling of any English word.

Volume 1: https://amzn.to/3l8Dkwl
Volume 2: https://amzn.to/3laodmv
Reading Supplement: https://amzn.to/3rF8QVH
Kindle: https://amzn.to/3ewRbLS
Teach a Student to Spell: Level 1: https://amzn.to/3dcNwkl
Teach a Student to Spell: Level 2: https://amzn.to/3xrDmFL
Teach a Student to Spell: Level 3: https://amzn.to/3z9MI9Z
Teach a Student to Spell: Level 4: https://amzn.to/3xWjVUW
Teach a Student to Spell: Level 5: https://amzn.to/3yoNTI1
Teach a Student to Spell: Level 6: https://amzn.to/3nIAYHd

Made in United States
North Haven, CT
08 April 2023

35065716R00128